THE HISTORY DEBATE

A HISTORY TODAY BOOK

THE HISTORY DEBATE

Edited by Juliet Gardiner

COLLINS & BROWN

First published in Great Britain in 1990
by Collins & Brown Limited
Mercury House
195 Knightsbridge
London SW7 1RE

A CIP catalogue record for this book
is available from the British Library

ISBN 1 85585 076 1

Phototypset by Falcon Typographic Art Ltd
Wallington and Edinburgh
Printed and bound in Great Britain by Richard Clay
(The Chaucer Press) Limited, Bungay

CONTENTS

INTRODUCTION

EVER SINCE HERODOTUS in the fifth century BC supposedly miscounted the Persian host there has been debate over the contents and purposes of history.

In the 1990s the Prime Minister, when faced with the imminent movement towards German unification and the threat of a hegemonic *Deutschmark*, called in a select handful of historians to advise her about that elusive phenomenon, the 'German national character' an aspect of the perception of the 'peculiarities of German history' – and was then criticised in some quarters for calling in the 'wrong' historians; earlier, when she had made a plea for a return to 'Victorian values', a fierce debate broke out as to what those values really were; when she opined on the advisability of the French Revolution in Paris on the 200th anniversary of the storming of the Bastille, she was accused not only of jeopardising the wider European ideal, but also of having a shaky grasp of French history; when the Labour frontbench spokesman on education defined his list of key historical facts which every child should know, he privileged the Match Girl's Strike over Waterloo.

Visiting what used to be called stately homes and are now called country houses, is one of the British family's favourite leisure pursuits, and whilst some commentators despair at the uncontextualised antiquarian information gathered on such trips, others are alarmed by the mushrooming of 'social history' museums which they see combining with the British magpie love of Victoriana to turn the past into a warm parlour of nostalgia.

Sensitivity to the need to conserve has extended well beyond the perfectly proportioned sweep of Georgian terraces to embrace the 'appropriate use' of former industrial workplaces – a concept informed by historical appreciation and knowledge. The pride which has puffed up the concept of 'civic trust' into one of 'national heritage' is distrusted by those who counterpoint it with anxieties about the 'commodification' of the past; the emphasis on the validity of experience and its expression in oral history has led to a belief that everyone has a purchase on the past, but the increasing demands of professional specialisation alienates this and one historian is not alone in his lament that soon 'we shall know more and more about less and less'.[1]

The call for a national history curriculum prompts the fear in some historians of a return to a celebratory 'drum and trumpet history', an emphasis on great men and great events with no space for the alternative narratives of women, the poor, blacks, in our country's history. Others are alarmed at the thought of children growing up unschooled in a chronology which enables them to chart their country's place in the world. The History Debate continues.

This debate has been focused recently by the plans of the present Conservative government to introduce a standardized national curriculum for schools throughout England and Wales. The National Curriculum History Working Group was set up in January 1989 by the Secretaries of State for Education and for Wales to make recommendations on attainment targets and programmes of study for history within the national curriculum for children between five and sixteen. The committee, chaired by Commander Saunders Watson, consisted of teachers of history in schools and universities, a couple of authors, a director of education, and the secretary of the Institute of Historical Research of the University of London. The final report, 205 pages of recommendations, was published in April 1990.

The debate occasioned by the setting up of the group, their interim report and by this final report, makes it hard to credit that less than a decade ago there was a very real possibility that history would cease to be a mainstream subject in British education at all. In addition to the formal and informal evidence taken from a wide range of experts and others in the field of history, nearly a thousand people responded to the interim report; those journalists anxious to proclaim their history credentials joining practising historians to rush into print under such headlines as 'Battle for the History Men', 'The Great Battle for History', 'Tories launch their biggest takeover bid for History'.

The report makes the committee's position clear in the opening sentence: 'History is a splendid subject for study at any age, but particularly in school. Children are by nature curious and the past provides a feast for that curiosity.'

The key to the wider debates comes next: 'The words "history" and "the past" are often used as synonyms, but there is an important distinction between "the past" which embraces everything that ever happened and "history" which chronicles, investigates and explains the past'. It is this selection of what is to be chronicled, this perception that whilst the past is unchanging, the interpretation of the past changes, that makes history such a contentious subject. The meanings of the interrogations form a domino theory; how history is taught shades its meaning into what history is taught and both conflate into why history is taught.

A brisk swathe is cut through the barren debate about facts *versus* skills: 'to have integrity the study of history must be grounded in a solid knowledge of the past: must employ vigorous historical method – the way in which historians carry out their task – and must involve a range of interpretations and explanations'. The report adds in bold type, for emphasis, a further warning, 'together, these elements make an organic whole: if any one of them is missing, the outcome is not history.'

The History Working Group is clear that the purpose of school history is 'to help [children to] understand the present in the context of the past; to arouse interest in the past; to help to give pupils a sense of identity; to help to give pupils an understanding of their cultural roots and shared inheritances; to contribute to pupils' knowledge and understanding of other countries and other cultures in the modern world; to train the mind by means of disciplined study; to introduce pupils to the distinctive methodology of historians; to enrich other areas of the curriculum and to prepare pupils for adult life'. Thus the course proposed must be 'challenging, relevant and interesting' – an aim clearly already achieved at the report stage if this is to be judged by the response from historians, teachers and the media.

The report has been broadly welcomed for being a fair and clear basis for history teaching in schools. But it has its critics: there are those like Robert Skidelsky who have complained about the lack of prescribed facts to be taught and have proposed an alternative, more 'factual' syllabus.[2] Keith Thomas has voiced concern with the excessive factual requirement: 'the exemplary information is sometimes intimidatingly formidable. That listed under history units for seven to eleven-year-olds includes the following: scrimshaw; shaduf; lynchets, hand querns; Sumerian cuneiform; Mary Jones and Quetzalcoatl . . . whatever this syllabus lacks it is not hard facts'.[3] It has been held to task for an idiosyncratic unevenness in coverage. In the following pages, Dr Janet Nelson argues the case for a more consistent approach to medieval history and warns of what Roger Mettam criticises as 'the minimal provision made for European history' so that children will not be told 'in an age of German reunification, that Germany is a more recent construction than the Crystal Palace, and that there has always been much disagreement about exactly which territories should, or should not be part of it.'[4] That is to suggest that in an admirable attempt to encourage children to be taught to chart the history of farther-flung parts of the world, and restrained by the Secretary of State's strictures that fifty per cent of the syllabus must be a concentration on British history, Europe, on the eve of 1992, has lost out.

It is the ambitious – or over-ambitious – nature of the report that has concerned many schoolteachers apprehensive of a prescription not easy to integrate with their existing history teaching which has evolved in the classroom in response to pupils' needs and abilities. The President of Corpus Christi College, Oxford, admonishes that if pupils have really learned to cope 'with increasing amounts of information; to show skill in selection; to use concepts and imagination in a disciplined way; to make comparisons and connections; to be aware of uncertainty; to be relevant and precise; to give explanations and summaries and make judgements; to plan, refine and communicate and to show independence of thought'[5] as the report requires, 'they would be capable of a First in Final Honours Schools let alone a pass at GCSE.'[6] Innovative and rigorous classroom teaching requires considerable resources both human and material, as Conrad Russell points out in his contribution to this book. School library shelves are not groaning with books on Mughal India, the Japanese Shogunate or sub-Saharan Africa since 1945. 'How many departments are currently involved in studies of seventh century Islam?' queries a history teacher in an Inner London comprehensive.[7] The demands on teachers will be heavy and the resources needed substantial if the generous and imaginative aspirations of the report are to be realised. Will the money for training and books be found for implementing the report with current curbs on educational spending?

But the History Debate encompasses a far wider dimension than an educationist's debate on the content of the school curriculum, or how and what history should be taught in polytechnics and universities. It is a metaphor for the debate about whose story Britain is anyway. History is seen to be national property and the controversy is predicated on the assumption – to which the French firmly subscribed after 1789 – that he who teaches the nation its history, captures its soul. That myopia in childhood is devilishly hard to correct in later life. It is the debate about the cultural agenda for Britain. As Martin Kettle wrote in *The Guardian*, 'It is about the right to dissent and debate not just history but a whole range of other assumptions'.[8] In theory a country's achievements are – and with recourse to history have been at least since the Franco-Prussian War – assessed in terms of scientific and technical education: in practice it is the teaching of history that has become the battleground.

There have been broad transforming influences in history in the past two decades; the growth of social history has validated new forms and new areas of enquiry, questioned assumptions about power and about change, and means that the 'great landmarks of British history', which the Prime Minister is insistent that children should recognise, have changed, since it does depend where you stand, what you see. An historian or pupil today is no longer simply Lord Acton's 'politician facing backwards': she or he has a wider, denser landscape in view.

These developments echo, and are themselves an echo of, social changes and expectations that can no more be reversed than can the exemplary lists of kings and queens and dates. The contributions to this book reflect the discussion about history teaching in schools which has been sharpened by the call for a national history curriculum: they also look at the wider implications of this debate. They look in different ways at the construction of a national identity; at the increasing scholasticism of some of the historical profession which finds its approach at odds with a population hungry to appreciate the past in accessible ways; at the making of a humanist education for our times and the ways in which the optic of historical enquiry has shifted over generations; at the place of Britain in the world and the comparative dimension of historical understanding; at the way imperial history has evolved and medieval history has been in danger of being misunderstood; at the necessary and valuable expertise of the historian and also how, on occasions, the historical profession has found itself marginalised through a reluctance to be utilitarian and useful in its insights and knowledge.

The History Working Group defines one of the key purposes of teaching history as being 'to prepare pupils for adult life. History gives pupils a framework of reference, opportunities for the informed use of leisure, and a critically sharpened intelligence with which to make sense of current affairs. History is a priceless preparation for citizenship, work and leisure.' No wonder setting the agenda for history is a political prize to be fought for. History is for life buffs and it's hardly surprising that this is a debate that will run and run.

JULIET GARDINER

NOTES

1. David Cannadine, 'British History: Past, Present – and Future?' *Past and Present* 116. August 1987.
2. R. Skidelsky and others, 'The National Curriculum. GCSE History – an alternative approach', May 24 1989.
3. 'The Future of the Past', *Times Literary Supplement,* June 8–14 1990.
4. 'No place for Europe', *Times Literary Supplement,* June 29 1990.
5. *National Curriculum. History Working Group. Final Report April 1990* (HMSO).
6. 'The Future of the Past'.
7. Paul Blum, '. . . and Present Imperfect', *Report*, March 1990 (The Assistant Masters' and Mistresses' Association).
8. Martin Kettle, 'The Great Battle for History', *The Guardian,* April 4 1990.

G. R. ELTON

"There are battalions of good reasons for continuing to study history, but not even those battalions can or should hide the fact that history is one of the most arduous, complex and simply difficult intellectual enterprises invented by man. "

NOWADAYS, HISTORIANS are quite often challenged to justify their existence: why do they study the past, and what contribution do they think they thereby make to the present? Such questions intersect with the supposed demonstration that in any case the past cannot be studied in any remotely objective way, so that all we get from the historian's labours are emanations of the present and of his personality. Between those who treat all discourse as a form of code requiring deconstruction (or whatever the vogue word happens to be at any given time), and those who maintain that no investigator can ever shed his load of inbuilt prejudices and preconceptions, the historian's ambition to get at a truth about the past is regularly torn to shreds.

As a matter of fact, it is not very difficult to dispose of the more rarefied objections. They have all been put together by people – philosophers and literary critics enamoured of refined theory – who have very little or absolutely no personal experience of writing history; they know nothing of the rigours of historical method and thus remain unaware of the control over the product exercise by a proper scholarly training in the use of historical sources and materials. Good historians, when disentangling the meaning of their sources, concentrate on two prescriptions designed to deal specifically with the sort of objections raised by philosophical and critical theory: they do not ask questions that have inbuilt answers, and they constantly regard their own preconceptions in order to minimise the effects these might have on the operation. So prepared, they then get down to asking the primary question of their materials – the question which at once removes it and them from the present into the context of the time studied: when, how, and for what purpose did those pieces of evidence come into existence? The answers to these crucial questions are strictly independent of the enquirer, and thus the possibility opens of an unprejudiced, open-minded and truly searching investigation.

All these precautions – which for a mind trained in a sound method are pretty well automatic – do not, of course, by themselves guarantee the discovery of the truth, though they enormously reduce the effect of distortion by observation. It is important to understand what is meant by truth in history, the more so because some philosophers, misled by and in their turn misleading some practitioners of the history of ideas, seem to suppose that historians seek for an absolute truth – for statements valid universally and at any time. Even the traditional believers, now much despised in the search for an objective historical reconstruction, never went so far as that. They wished to discover what and how and why things had happened, and they held it possible to arrive at a final conclusion in that quest, but they never supposed that the truths they worked out stood as universally valid and apart from the series of events within which they were discovered. In fact, the historian's truth is a very simple thing to describe, though a devilishly hard thing to pursue. It is that which actually happened. That something actually happened will surely be accepted by everyone who has ever undergone experience – who has lived, acted, been acted upon, and possibly has even thought. By the same token, everyone who has done these things or witnessed them in others knows perfectly well that extracting them from the past and giving them convincing shape is not only a very difficult task but also an unending one. The historian has some affinities with the writer of imaginative fiction, even if, contrary to Aristotle, he feels himself intellectually superior to his distant cousin. The chief difference between them lies in the fact that the story the historian tells did actually once happen and cannot be altered by invention, from which it also follows that since in its totality it will never be recovered all efforts lead only to incomplete results and leave the way open for further investigation and reconstruction.

The problem of truth in history therefore constitutes an essentially impossible conundrum. We know that that truth lies behind the curtain that separates us from the event and its contents; we know we can lift the curtain here and there and thus see parts of the truth; and we know that we shall never see it all or see it in ways that prove totally convincing to everyone. These incompletenesses have nothing to do with any possible injection of the investigator's personal beliefs or prejudices into the investigation, nor with such things as the obscurity of meaning, language as a code, or any of the other refinements which distinguish critical theory and remove it so far from real experience. It is a simple condition of the enterprise created by its massive difficulty and aggravated by the patchy and ambiguous evidence which the past has deposited for present use. Allowing for all this, it is no wonder that so many people, scholars among them, hope to render the patchy ambiguity of the past more complete and perhaps more useful by subordinating it to general schemes of thought and interpretation which sculpt the evidence rather than derive from it. But this escape mechanism destroys the truth of history by wrapping it up in convenient fictions: it does elevate the personal preferences of the historian above the restraints imposed by the desire to seek the truth.

If the reality of history remains for ever beyond the edge of the horizon, or at any rate can be only in part and approximately reconstructed, is the enterprise worth pursuing? Why should we devote time, effort and much ingenuity to labours which must be defined as for ever incomplete? Leaving aside the sheer attraction of studying the past, there are three possible answers to this question – accepting that the answer 'no' is automatically excluded from a piece appearing in this collection. The reason most commonly advanced is that history teaches lessons – that we can and should learn from history. The notion certainly contains a truth, but it does not mean what most people seem to suppose it means. General opinion holds that if we understand how a present situation came about we can the more readily forecast, or indeed determine, how it will develop into the future. Extreme views on this topic suppose that the past, properly analysed, will reveal general laws of human behaviour and experience which can then be applied forward. Such law-creating concepts have always attracted those who cannot bear uncertainty, or alternatively those who wish to impose their own preferred developments upon other people. The most recent and most current such set of beliefs, supposedly scientific, are the tenets of Marxism which explains the past as a struggle between classes and forecasts – or at least used to forecast until the other day – an end to the process in the victory of the classless society. One might suppose that the events of 1989, when all those progressive socialist (Marxist) structures in Eastern Europe vanished in a trice might put an end to those imaginative dreams, but believers are not so easily swayed from their convictions, and I expect a Marxist revival quite soon, especially in those countries that never experienced a communist regime. More serious for the proposition that we can and should learn from the past about the future is the fact that so far no one (to my knowledge) has claimed to have foreseen the drastic collapse of one such regime after another.

Even less predestinarian convictions based upon a knowledge of the past have rarely supported the hope that history teaches lessons for action in the present. Some of the best of scholars have in their day proved incapable of really assessing the situation in which they found themselves or of advising a sensible (and successful) course of future action. Nineteenth-century German historians, for instance, under the influence of Hegel, believed the nation-state to be not only a fact of life but also the predestined end of human organisation; they came to endow it with virtues saintly and inspirational, quite independent of its actual behaviour. On the other side, liberal and more-than-liberal enthusiasts have several times placed their national structures within supra-national bodies supposedly proven by history to be in the ascendant: they turned out to be as wrong as all the rest. One striking example of the comprehensive error involved in learning from history was provided by the dissolution of colonial empires after the Second World War. Those changes were represented as historically inevitable (an unproven assertion), as morally necessary (which has little to do with historical understanding), and as humanly beneficial, a verdict that the millions of dead in the wake of European withdrawal might be thought to call in question. The fact of decolonisation in no way demonstrates the supposed lessons of history which did not support the actions taken even when called in witness.

None of this, however, means (our second answer) that one cannot learn from history. The error has lain in the human inclination to decide upon the lesson first and then to find support for it in the study of the past. Furthermore, too often the shape of that past has itself been determined by presentist desires and concerns. R.H. Tawney, to take one example, misrepresented an era of supposed early capitalism in the sixteenth century because he wished to display the roots of a system which he was trying to dismantle. The whole Nazi myth of Aryan triumph easily created a historical background that seemed to give it learned reality. There is no need to go on about this: most commonly the so-called lessons of history derive from myths useful to a policy or viewpoint adopted in the present, those myths then being foisted upon the past.

Yet there are real lessons to be learned from history. An acquaintance with the past studied for its own sake, with primary regard for those people dead and gone, will indeed teach a great deal about human behaviour, human action and human potential. What it will teach above all is the unpredictability of the human animal. The lesson of history hammers home the weight of the unexpected, the contingent, the totally surprising, within a generally somewhat humdrum setting of the reasonably expectable and the arguably consequential. A dispassionate study of the past offers the opportunity of enlarging one's area of experience beyond anything that can be obtained in one's own life. History being about people, it teaches what people are like and what they are capable of doing, without creating stereotypes or precisely forecasting what will happen. Learning these lessons means growing up, in as much as it means putting the reality of other people ahead of the self-centred demands which characterise the adolescent. And if I am told that this is simply praise for the conservative as against the radical temperament, I would in part deny the charge but also in part accept it. Being adult means being able to accept people and things as they really are, whereas the young idealist can see only the call for changes prescribed by radical faiths and can ignore the blood spilt.

Now to the third answer to our original question. From the use of history as the teacher of what humanity is really like there springs a more specific usefulness. A historical training offers a special chance to develop the critical faculties in a practical and comprehensive way. Historians are trained to look critically at the two stages of their own operations. They must learn to understand their evidential material by probing behind surface appearances and biased claims. And they must learn to treat both their own and other people's explanatory structures with constructive critiques because they know that the absence of final and provable certainty often leaves room for doubts and alterations. These are skills well worth applying in the daily present. Whereas the theory-based sciences concerned with human potential and action – disciplines such as economics or sociology – seek to solve questions by using generalisations backed by selective groundwork, historians are (or should be) by training and experience sceptical of all such constructs. This does not mean that they always disbelieve or destroy them; it does mean that they will not accept them untested, as articles of faith. I am here, of course, talking about historians who have not fallen prey to the social-science ambitions of universalisation and prophecy – real historians immersed in the realities of the past and conscious of the particularity of human beings. To the age in which they live they can offer a species of laboratory for testing the propositions and plans put up by the scientists. This offer is precious at any time but especially called for in days when such propositions and plans sprout in profusion and are proclaimed with the confidence bred from ignorance. A good historian knows that no answer can stand unchallenged merely because it is pronounced by someone claiming the authority of a faith or even an expertise: authority is a word that the properly trained historian simply should not allow to enter his mind. A good historian also knows that however much he may challenge such answers he may well fail to prevent humanity from rushing down the steep slopes of faith. If we are still seeking for 'relevance' in historical studies we should be well advised to find it in the sceptical review, based on an understanding of the past, of all those confident solutions offered for present troubles and future hopes.

If, however, historians are to carry out this task of being humanity's charitable watchdog they need to keep one thing firmly in mind. They need to keep open the lines of communication to non-historians (including social scientists). If I am right about the services the trained and skilled historian can render outside the reservations of his profession, it follows that he must make himself comprehensible to all sorts of women and men; he must learn to talk to those who, though not fellow scholars, are willing to listen. This may appear to be an obvious necessity and many seem to suppose that it poses no very serious difficulties, but in fact the unquestioned crisis in historical studies gathers far more around this issue than around the dangers of preconditioned reflexes, inbuilt prejudices, over-ready assumptions, or any of the philosophical doubts that have been put in the way of the historian. All those can in large measure be overcome by training and application – by learning the trade. Unfortunately, however, the very circumstances of learning the trade appear to operate against ready communication. As the investigator digs into the depths, and as he rightly dissects his evidence with the help of insights and techniques developed in other human disciplines, he meets, and is only too likely to be swallowed up by, the burdensome problems of concepts and answers expressed in a language which the generality does not know. An historian's disappearance into the distant world of mathematics (graphs and statistics) – what has come to be called cliometrics – is only the extreme case of this affliction. Jargon proliferates around learning; it has always done so, and nowadays does so the more readily because so much of the advanced work is done not in English but in American.

It is also the case that the labouring scholar, anxious to offer no hostages to fortune, will find bushels of obscurity under which to hide the light of his learning. Every historian worthy of the name is well aware that what he cannot put before his readers are absolute truths, verifiable by supposedly scientific methods; he knows that if he has anything at all to say that merits attention he will call forth doubt, contradiction, perhaps furious hostility. Being by nature a peaceful creature, and preferring to browse in his field without constantly stubbing his toes on steel-traps put there by enemies – called critics – he comes to think it a good idea to wrap every statement in reservations, limitations and apologies which will, he hopes, form thickets of cover into which to withdraw at the approach of hostile steps.

Between them, the jargon promoted by specialisation (especially the intrusion of theory) and the muffler wrapped around the face to ward off evil eyes, erect barriers between the historian and his readers which vary from mere bewilderment to solid boredom. The remedies respond to the affliction. Precision and clarity of language ward off jargon: the writer should use real words set in genuine sentences. And open-minded exposition of arguments and conclusions overcomes obscurity. We must treat writing as yet another skill to be acquired. Here, however, a further danger lies in wait: the historian can be tempted into the artificiality of so-called good writing, into pretentiousness, into the supposed colour of mere prejudice. Facility has its own perils; writing history is as difficult as is the unravelling of the past. But both tasks must be conscientiously discharged if the historian is to do his proper duty to the past and render his proper service to the present. In short, there are battalions of good reasons for continuing to study history, but not even those battalions can or should hide the fact that history is one of the most arduous, complex, and simply difficult intellectual enterprises invented by man. Studying the human animal, the historian has reason for remembering the labours of Hercules and Sisyphus.

It is therefore important also to remember that studying history is exciting, rewarding, a splendid way to pass the time. Actually, it is fun.

ROY PORTER

"For the health of history it is crucial that historians no less, perhaps, than the acting profession, recognise their responsibilities to meeting public needs (and equally their duty to cultivate good communication skills). Otherwise we will be treated with deserved contempt, as being guilty of a prissy dereliction of duty."

OVER THE LAST decade, the government has decided to take a stand on the teaching of history. History must be relevant, history must confirm a sense of British identity, history should be taught on tangible grids of dates and facts. These directives raise two questions. First, what is the *purpose* of history? (The official assumption is that good history is usable history.) Second, what should be the *contents* of history? (Here the Education Secretary has favoured teaching a common core focusing upon some supposed common national heritage.)

Academic historians and history teachers have reacted alike in a hostile manner to these directives from Above; don't we all hanker after some ideal of *Lernfreiheit* and *Lehrfreiheit*? Other contributors to this volume explain why the government's proposals are retrograde; I share their views. Here I wish, however, to argue, more provocatively, that if we historians find ourselves in the humiliating position of being told how to do our own job, at bottom we have only ourselves to blame (and doubly so, if we can't see why this is the case). How so?

For over a century, historians have been proclaiming their independence. They are scholars, investigators, researchers. They probe into the past with the same objectivity, neutrality, disinterest, the same Olympian superiority to prejudice, as a scientist peering down his microscope at a bacteria culture on a Petri dish. They are animated by pure love of truth, and labouring to advance knowledge.

History, the object of their inquiry, is a corpus of ancient manuscripts, official records, and material objects, which by the meticulous cultivation of increasingly exacting scholarly techniques, can be made to yield more accurate (or at least less erroneous) findings. If the limitations of the sources prevent full reconstruction of the truth, we can at least better know what we can't know, and dynamite old myths (Newton did not discover gravity by watching an apple fall; and so forth).

Or, perhaps – and this is the more radical view that has gained a purchase – history really *is* nothing more than a heap of documents, remains, fragments. The very notion of a coherent past – a domain in which it would be possible to reconstruct causes and effects, motives, intentions, and personalities, the relations between actions and outcomes – has been subjected to searching scrutiny: philosophical, methodological, and epistemological. History, it is today widely touted, is, after all, just in the eye of the beholder. All is subjective, primarily a projection of the researcher's prejudices (and as Freudians would insist, these are typically unconscious, and so hidden from historians themselves). History is thus trapped in an eternal present, doomed to fabricating mythical pasts.

The development of such self-critical perspectives certainly represents real triumphs of methodological rigour and self-awareness. Historians are nothing if not critical these days, and their research methods have become notably more sophisticated and stringent. Only a fool, nostalgically wallowing in history's past, would want to revert to previous versions. We are all professionals now.

Professionals, as is well known, boast their own exclusive technical skills, their own definitions of reality, and, above all, exercise monopolistic control over their turf. With history, this may be a very mixed blessing. Professionalization has assuredly demolished old readings of the past. In some cases, it's less clear what's been put in their place, except a series of 'Keep Out: No Trespassers' notices to outsiders, and, not least, to fellow researchers. For with professionalization has come specialization – at its worst, knowing more and more about less and less. Each historian cultivates his or her own patch, defending it against poachers. The old common fields of history are enclosed into a multiplicity of privately-owned periods and problems, fenced off against each other. 'It's not my subject, not my period', becomes the legitimate excuse of the myopic ultra-specialist, when asked to peer over the hedge.

The result can often be confusing and negative. Take the Industrial Revolution. Or rather the supposed, or so-called, or 'mythical', Industrial Revolution. Vast scholarly labours have been invested these last fifty years in dissecting this beast. It's been noted that no one called it a 'revolution' until quite late in the nineteenth century. The motives of those who thus retrospectively labelled it have been probed. Thousands of indices of economic growth (investment, output, horse-power, etc.) have been constructed; and each, in succession, has been shown to fail to reveal a moment of decisive transition, that sudden break in the historical process which would allow us to say, decisively, 'here is the revolutionary leap'. In any case, the philosophers of history have been asking: what is a revolution? They have explained that the term is just a metaphor, smuggled in from its earlier, original meanings (the rotation of a wheel, the orbit of a planet); it has been habitually deployed by scholars of a particular ideological slant, above all, Marxists, with their stake in revolutions past to guarantee revolutions present and future.

Thus, like the Cheshire Cat, the Industrial Revolution has been fading away before our very eyes (alongside other revolutions, such as the English Revolution, or the Scientific Revolution). Yet it has left a smile. Any intelligent, well-informed observer with a modicum of practical experience of the First and Third Worlds knows there *was* an Industrial Revolution, and knows in broad terms what it entailed (mechanization, artificial power, mass-production of commodities, the development of consumerism) – and such an observer may well be contemptuous of academics who dispute that self-evident fact. Historians must, of course, have scruples and a passion for precision. But the scholar who cannot also deploy broad commonsensical truths, can't see the wood for the trees, is rather like the myopic scientist who might ascertain that his specimen contains a certain percentage of water, fat, tissue, and bones, but is unable to recognize an elephant.

The old past is dead. Historians have killed it off, and that's no bad thing. The trouble is that, too often, all that have replaced it are fiendishly technical, dry-as-dust manipulations of data, an accent upon minute periodization, a fragmentation of topics, and – worse still – a disposition, in the name of scholarly integrity, to deny that history possesses any patterns, grand transitions, or lessons (because the scrupulous scholar cannot *prove* them, or denies that it's his job to make value-judgments). Faced with this pedantic, professional triumph of methods over meanings, no wonder the public votes with its feet, and reads historical novels, or non-academic, non-professional historians; or, buys up greedily when, comparatively rarely, professional historians *do* write books showing the wider sweep and coherence of the destinies of nations, as, for instance, Paul Kennedy's *Rise and Fall of the Great Powers* (1988), which struck chords with countless readers pondering the current crumbling of the Soviet Empire.

It is not unusual for scholars to go in for soul-searching and breast-beating. What I am describing, however, is more than the niggle of the neglected. It is a matter of recognizing a loss of mission and purpose amongst the historical community. As Sir John Plumb's

The Death of the Past pointed out, some twenty years ago, it is at their own peril that academic historians neglect the educated public. They cut themselves off from their own audience, and in the process abandon the general reader or viewer to whatever quack historians and biographers will be sucked in to fill the vacuum.

Far from being prophets crying in the wilderness, truth to tell, historians seemed no longer to have anything to say. Plumb argued this crisis of the historians was symptomatic of a deeper crisis in our culture's perception of history. Time was when it was self-evident that the past was relevant to the present: age meant wisdom, every-one followed customs, politicians and lawyers relied on precedents, the old ways conferred craft skills, know-how was handed down from father to son, mother to daughter. Thus the past dictated to the present, and the value of a working knowledge of the past was universally appreciated.

But, Plumb observed, things were fast changing. Not just because scholars, by scrutinizing fragments under a microscope, had aban-doned a commitment to resurrecting living history; but because the rate of economic, technical, and social change had become so rapid in our society as to condemn the past to the status of a museum piece, irrelevant, at best merely picturesque, fit only for servicing the tourist trade. Various scholars – David Lowenthal in his *The Past is a Foreign Country* (1985), Patrick White, in his *On Living in an Old Country* (1985), and Donald Horne, in his *The Great Museum: the Representation of History* (1984) – have shown how the past has become relegated to 'heritage', and have pointed to the dangers of such nostalgic euthanasia.

It is understandable that commentators convinced themselves that the past was becoming obsolete, except as a form of costume drama. Especially in the 1960s, the accent was on youth, rebellion, and ridicule of the fuddy-duddy. But overall, the judgement is mistaken. For one thing, the Prime Minister herself, in calling for a restoration of Victorian values, underlined the relevance of the past, as she saw it, to the present (a pity her knowledge of what actually constituted Victorian values proved so shaky). More generally, as is evident from the popularity of historical programmes on radio and television, of local history museums, theme parks, stately homes, national monu-ments, and the like, an age of change does not so much erode, but actually intensifies, the need to root the present back in the past, to establish the stories of one's origins, and the line of one's life. Television broadcasts on historical subjects – from documentaries about the Great War to the tales of everyday objects like deodorants and condoms – capture the public imagination.

A rather disoriented generation thus seeks enlightenment about its own identity. But the hunger for history is sometimes more specific still. In times of perplexity and crisis, to what do people turn when needing guidelines for informed debate, decisions and actions? They look to history. Of this, the most obvious, and perhaps the most crucial, instance over the last decade, has been the AIDS threat.

AIDS cases began to appear in this country in the early 1980s. By the mid-eighties, it was recognized that an epidemic was on the cards, possibly on the scale developing in the United States and visible in Central Africa. The micro-organic source of the disease remained disputed. No one knew exactly its precise pathways of transmission, its likely prognosis; certainly no cure was in sight. Public concern was growing; in some quarters, panic and hysteria arose, or were fanned. Police chiefs and the tabloid press were telling us AIDS was an act of God, divine wrath retaliating against permissiveness in general and above all the unnatural practices of gays.

What was going to develop, what was to be done? No one in the Department of Health and Social Security (DHSS) quite knew, partly because former great epidemics – smallpox, typhoid, cholera – had so long since been controlled or eradicated in the West; first-hand experience of managing mass outbreaks of killer diseases has disappeared. Suddenly everyone was turning to history for the answers. Was AIDS unique? Had there had been comparable diseases in earlier centuries, decimating epidemics in the past? If so, how had societies responded? What measures had been taken by earlier regimes to contain contagion? Had legislation been enacted? How had the public health apparatus operated? Had preventive measures be taken? What were they? Had they worked? Had the spread of such diseases been limited? Not least: what finally had happened?

History had some answers. Europe, as historians were able to point out, had, of course, been swept by numerous great pestilences, from the Black Death in the mid-fourteenth century, through repeated outbreaks of Bubonic Plague right up to the early eighteenth century. Smallpox, typhus, etc. had been virulent into the nineteenth century; cholera had visited Europe and America in great waves in the Victorian era; and, most appositely to the case of AIDS, syphilis had been endemic since the close of the fifteenth century, perhaps brought back from the new world by Columbus as part of what has been called the 'Columbian Exchange'.

At their height, these diseases had had no known cure. For that very reason (as historians blessed with hindsight could judge), panics had erupted, Divine Judgment had been invoked, sinners called to repentance, victims vilified, and vulnerable minorities scapegoated and persecuted. Indeed, as Richard Davenport-Hines's *Sex, Death and Punishment* (1990) has argued, the advent of the mysterious new disease of syphilis – agonizingly painful, disfiguring, often fatal, and quite visibly sexually-transmitted – perhaps produced a perduring and deeply-ingrained sexual puritanism and punitiveness in our culture.

So what had been done? Historians were able to show that Western polities had very extensive experience of responding to deadly plagues. In the Renaissance, major Italian cities, Venice above all, had initiated ferocious quarantines, especially against shipping and merchants. (Evidently, we were not the first era to contemplate the need for strict action to safeguard the public health.) Other studies, notably Paul Slack's *The Impact of Plague in Tudor and Stuart England* (1985), had traced the often acrimonious debates conducted in sixteenth- and seventeenth-century Britain over the necessity or advisability of coercive public measures against plague suspects and victims. The authorities tended to argue in their favour, to preserve public order and stop the spread of disease, whereas many puritans, concerned for the sufferers, took the opposite view, on the grounds that house-confinement was in breach of the Christian duties of charity and neighbourliness. Providence would strike and spare where it would.

In the eighteenth century, the arguments about quarantine and compulsion took a more economic and secular turn: what would be the cost, in terms of commercial disruption, of abrogating the freedom of individuals to come and go as they pleased? In the nineteenth century, the issue of personal rights and common interests acquired a more principled flavour in the philosophies of *laissez-faire* and individualism, as advanced, for instance, by John Stuart Mill: might not state intervention – e.g. compulsory smallpox vaccination – breach the sacred freedom of the person? Nevertheless, the Victorian age proved a great period of public health mobilization, with the introduction of the concept of notifiable diseases and the Contagious Diseases Acts.

Yet what confusion resulted! Passed in the 1860s, these Acts empowered authorities under certain circumstances to inspect prostitutes for sexually transmitted diseases, and, if found infected, to confine them till cured. The Acts provoked storms of protests – amongst feminists, libertarians, moral hard-liners (for whom they seemed to be condoning vice, by providing safe sex), and not least, many doctors, who found the idea of being turned into a state police obnoxious. The Acts were repealed, and thereafter (and to this day) the operation of venereal disease facilities has proceeded in Britain, unlike many other countries, on a voluntary basis, on the assumption, apparently borne out by experience, that compulsion actually hinders treatment.

In the mid-eighties, medical historians surveyed afresh the various means societies had used to cope with pestilences. Whole books were devoted to the subject, for instance *AIDS; The Burdens of History,* edited by Elizabeth Fee and Daniel Fox (1988). Conferences organized by the medical profession and by AIDS support groups, working parties and committees, urgently attempting to come to terms with the AIDS crisis, called upon historians for information, interpretation, and advice. Various academics – as the present writer can testify – were summoned by the DHSS to supply dossiers of historical data. These materials, it appears, were digested and incorporated into Ministry documents, official speeches, and, perhaps, policy.

The story of the forging of the British government's response to AIDS remains to be written. But it is at least plausible to argue that the policy which emerged (one of avoiding the coercive legislation widely being demanded, and instead encouraging education, publicity, and voluntary initiatives) was formulated to some degree in the light of historical evidence and analyses of past epidemic experience. It is too early to judge, but if it turns out that this policy proves reasonably successful in alerting people to the dangers of HIV-infection, without resort to the punitive measures advocated in some quarters, historical awareness may have played some modest part in this success. Beyond doubt, the mere knowledge that similar threats had been faced in the past afforded some reassurance in a climate of opinion always threatening to become panicky.

Two conclusions may be drawn. *First,* to ensure informed and intelligent discussion and decision-making on many public issues, perspectives on the past seem invaluable. This is true in a general way: we need a broad sense of history, a grasp of how groups interact, an appreciation of the ambiguous dialectics between intentions and consequences, policy and practice. Sometimes, it applies more specifically too. Cases like the AIDS crisis benefit from analyses of parallel situations in the past. Abstract principles may be less helpful than the concrete evidence of precedent and example.

The AIDS crisis has revealed the public looking to history for information and guidance. Hence it is doubly important that historians don't pen themselves up in ivory towers, spinning sophisticated philosophical denials of the continuities between past and present, and insisting that history teaches nothing (except that it teaches nothing). Renaissance scholars believed the historian must necessarily be a good citizen. We might do well to learn that lesson.

Second – and this goes back to the issue raised right at the beginning of this discussion, concerning the proper *contents* of history – the AIDS example shows how important it is that we cultivate a catholic sense of what kinds of history matter, what should be taught, in what fields research should be encouraged. The educational policies of the Thatcher government have sought to bring history-teaching back to a highly traditionalist curriculum, concentrating upon the political history and traditions of the United Kingdom.

Let us not deny that, done properly, this would provide a valuable body of knowledge and insights. One of my responsibilities as lecturer at the Wellcome Institute for the History of Medicine is to teach medical students from the various London hospitals. Who would deny that doctors-to-be should have a grasp of the political institutions of their own country, one facet of which is obviously a sense of the historical evolution of the Welfare State, including the NHS? But I am often shocked to find how few of them have studied *any* twentieth-century British political history at school (and gratified to discover how keen they are to learn).

Nevertheless, it is vital not to create a climate of opinion in which British political history is all that it is thought worth teaching in schools and to future teachers, worth researching and supporting research into. Citizens need to know about the political institutions which shape their lives. But they also need to be able to make well-informed judgments about the worlds of work, of the family, of social and moral values. People need sound bases upon which to shape their own opinions, and understand the views of others. The young must be able to deal confidently with questions about sex and gender roles, about rich and poor, black and white, old and young, (ex-)Christian and non-Christian, if they are to be able to flourish in a complex, fast-changing, multi-cultural society.

One of the best ways of learning to cope with challenging situations lies in awareness that comparable challenges have been faced before (e.g. of the need to create a pluralist society out of disparate elements), and by relating to predecessors fighting similar fights (for instance, Victorian feminists). None of this is possible without ready access to specialist knowledge: say, the findings of women's history, or research into race relations, or (as I've been indicating) into the history of medicine. I referred earlier, rather deprecatingly, to scholarly specialisation. Narrowness *is* a vice. Specialization is, however, necessary, but it needs to be tempered with compensating strengths. Thus those who focus down upon a small field might need to embrace a long time-span.

For the health of history, it is crucial that historians, no less, perhaps, than the acting profession, recognize their responsibilities to meeting public needs (and equally their duty to cultivate good communication skills). Otherwise we will be treated with deserved contempt, as being guilty of a prissy dereliction of duty. The AIDS crisis is only one of many issues where the public and politicians look to history for illumination, ideas, and help. It is up to us not to let them down.

KEITH ROBBINS

"It is significant that the Secretary of State, in calling for more 'British history' presupposed that it was self-evident what 'British history' was."

IN 1940, ·WHILE plunging into a sea of changes, novelties and inventions', Herbert Butterfield saw an England which 'resumed contact with her traditions and threw out ropes to the preceding generations, as though in time of danger it was a good thing not to lose touch with the convoy'. At a time when survival was in doubt, he thought he discerned the process by which, over a long period, partisan attitudes and ideologies became absorbed into a tradition that was nation-wide. Englishmen acquired and handed down from one generation to another a characteristic method and policy. It was 'a system which we can call our own'. We were 'a country of traditions' and there remained 'a living continuity in our history'. Immersion in the history of those traditions in turn sustained them.

Half a century later, this stirring picture looks rather remote. Political leaders in 1940 were able persuasively to draw upon the bank of the past in order to fortify the spirit of a nation at war. In 1990, however, the 'sea of changes, novelties and inventions' has become ever more disruptive. Traditions, whether 'real' or 'invented', have been threatened by the corrosive impact of global images. It has become increasingly difficult to know how the 'English convoy' was composed and in what direction, under Providence, it was headed. Stanley Baldwin's Englishman of 1924 was a being made for a time of crisis. He was serene in difficulties, ruthless in action and persistent to the death, though he might not look ahead sufficiently. It was these gifts which enabled the Englishman to make England and the Empire what it was. These were words addressed to the Royal Society of St George in the year of the British Empire Exhibition. In 1990 of course the Empire is no more. The decades of its demise have precipitated a cultural/historiographical crisis through which we are currently living. Images of national identity and character are challenged and manipulated – not for the first time – in an attempt to make sense of the present.

Even into the 1960s, at least in the mindset of the generation which held political power, 'British history' had been traditionally conceived, for more than a century, as reaching its ultimate expression in 'Greater Britain'. Despite all its faults and imperfections, the British Empire was the greatest achievement of the extraordinary islanders. The patron saint of sailors, Baldwin remarked, was surely the most suitable patron saint for men of English stock. The insular gypsies had created a world-wide fellowship celebrated by historians who were themselves at home in this scattered network of Britishness. Charles Carrington, for example, was born in the Midlands two years before the Boer War, brought up in New Zealand, educated at Oxford and taught, for a time, at Haileybury. He gave his allegiance to Rudyard Kipling and produced two volumes on *The British Overseas* in 1950. By the time of his death, in 1990, the concept of 'the British overseas', in the sense of a community of people girdling the globe, seemed irremediably obsolete. Even the Commonwealth had ceased to be British.

An historiography which both expressed and reinforced a certain self-perception cannot be easily shrugged off. It is equally apparent, however, that it has little purchase on the contemporary world, but it must be said that historians have been no better than policy-makers in general in finding a new framework within which they conceive the nature and scope of 'British history'. Historians too have lost an empire and not found a role. Of course, many of them have thrown off the imperial mantle with joy. They have devoted themselves to the ever more profound examination of discrete and self-contained topics without bothering their heads over longer-term problems of 'national destiny'. They are rather annoyed that governments and people still want to bother with such things. The debate about 'History in the National Curriculum' which has reverberated around the reports of the History Working Group has made it plain, however, that 'British history' still matters. The Secretary of State, in receiving the interim report, expressed his disquiet that the programmes of study recommended by the Group provided for less than 50 per cent of time to be given to British history in the upper age range. He wanted the British experience to be given a sharper focus. The guidance to the Chairman had stipulated that the programmes of study should have the history of Britain 'at the core'. In its final report, the Working Group made alterations which it hoped would meet the view expressed by the minister. In doing so, however, it took the view that to place British history at the centre of its proposals did not mean that British history was, or had to be, 'pivotal'.

It is significant that the Secretary of State, in calling for more 'British history' presupposed that it was self-evident what 'British history' was. It was simply a matter of increasing the ration of a commodity which was readily labelled and could be taken off the shelf without difficulty. It is my contention, however, that this is so no longer. I would not myself take issue with the view that British history should have a central role in school. It seems to me entirely defensible that a society should attach particular significance to unravelling, in appropriate modes and at appropriate levels, the complexity of its own past. There are 'signposts', 'markers' or 'landmarks' to which we collectively relate and which help the cohesion of that society. The danger arises only if the 'signposts' are transformed into exclusive 'badges' and 'Britishness' is thought to be embodied most purely in a particular tradition. We should not draw the conclusion, simply because 'British history' might conceivably be manipulated for some particular political purpose, that it should become almost insignificant in a syllabus which should have 'the world' at the centre and confine 'British history' to a walk-on part in a global documentary. 'British history' lies all around us in our infancy and we can sense the significance of landscape and buildings in an intimate fashion in a way that is not possible if we seek to sail in a global ship without anchorage in a particular place through time.

On the other hand, a British history that simply looked in upon itself would be neither stimulating nor satisfying. Rootedness must be matched by an awareness of external diversity. The problem is to find the right balance and context as 'British history' moves from being a self-contained universe in itself to a different order of existence in the late-twentieth century. The problems of adjustment and context in historiography in this respect mirror those of British society at large. The future, in this respect, remains unclear but certain trends are discernible.

It would be unlikely, for example, that even an English male historian would commit himself to a book on *The Englishman and His History* as Butterfield did to a people in crisis in 1944. It may in part be a further aspect of the demise of Empire, but historians now are generally more alert to the complexity of the United Kingdom and 'Britishness'. Now that the diversion of overseas expansion is over, we turn again to the difficult relationships within these islands. How many nations are we and what political arrangements best accommodate our unity and diversity? What does 'Britain' mean? The angle of vision has shifted. The past of 'Britain' no longer seems a mere prelude – a rather lengthy prelude! – to the overseas enterprise. As we look at the British Isles in the middle ages, for example through the eyes of historians like Robin Frame or Rees Davies, we can see patterns of alignment and activity which have implications for the present and the future. It is, perhaps, a truncated notion of 'British history' but, as John Pocock puts it, in many respects we are dealing with what for many is conceptually a 'new subject'. The final report of the Working Group comes to terms with this problem and opportunity, though it recognizes that the books at an appropriate level often still need to be written, so pervasive is the legacy of a certain type of Anglo-centric historiography. It is also a sign of the times that there has been a History Committee for Wales which has suggested British history programmes of study which have accorded the history of Wales a particular prominence. The Committee argues that Welsh history is far more than a regional exemplification of British history. It stresses, however, that to insist on the separate identity of Wales is not to claim that the history of Wales should be taught in isolation. It provides examples of the way in which the place of Wales within the history of the British Isles as a whole can be studied. In Northern Ireland, too, historians are grappling with the problems of providing a history which 'places' Northern Ireland both within Ireland and in 'Britain'. In Scotland, too, the same issue has been tackled, though without the formal interlocking enshrined in the delivery of the England/Wales reports. There is, therefore, something of a paradox in the fact that a 'National Curriculum' in history will probably produce a curriculum of nations which will recognize explicitly both the unity and the diversity of the British Isles. It is a process not without wide public implications, not least for the Republic of Ireland.

Historians involved in this programme of discussion and debate, whatever may be the final form of the curriculum when it comes to be taught in the United Kingdom, cannot but be aware of the ramifications of their conclusions. The shaping of content and the framework of argument are themselves political decisions, in the widest sense of the term. The historiographical tendencies which have been discusssed have intrinsic justification but they also reflect the deeper processes of political change which have also been alluded to. Who is pushing and who is pulling?

In no area is this more apparent than in the vexed question of the relationship between 'British history' and 'European history'. Throughout the school system, and frequently in higher education, a firm divide exists between the terrain of 'British' and 'European': often different books, different lessons, different teachers. Of course, it is frequently stated that there are 'links' between the two, but the extent to which they are systematically explored varies considerably from institution to institution. The 'public historical mind' has been conditioned to the notion that two discrete areas of study are involved, and this divorce again has serious implications in the very late twentieth century. The extent of the gulf is not paralleled in any other European country. Countries differ in the extent to which they do accord specific priority to 'national' history but, whatever the balance, it is national history as a part of European history rather than set against it as tends to be the case in the United Kingdom. The History Working Group appears to have been uncertain how to proceed. A ministerial injunction specifically to ensure at least fifty per cent 'British history' seemed to preclude the possibility of a solution along the lines of a 'European history' into which British history could be slotted. Even without that guideline, the task of doing so is formidably difficult. The final report, in commenting on the history of countries other than Britain, states that there are good reasons for studying European history in particular. It goes so far as to say that 'Britain is part of Europe' and that its history has helped to shape and been shaped by that of its European neighbours. Since political ties with Western Europe are 'growing stronger' it argues that it is important that British pupils should understand 'the European past'. It is significant that the report does not speak of 'their European past'. The options perpetuate the dichotomy by providing, for example, the consideration of twentieth-century Britain and of Europe in separate compartments. I would argue, on the contrary, that there is no such thing as 'the European past'. British history shares in the complexity of Europe's many pasts, sometimes to greater, sometimes to lesser degree – but in this respect does not vastly differ from the history of other European national histories. It is this issue which ought to be central to providing a 'Britain-in-Europe' historiography which appears to meet the needs of the hour.

Such a statement may seem to some to be mere pandering to 'presentism'. Of course, to argue for the authenticity of British history within the dynamic history of contemporary Europe has its dangers. It could lead to a conscious and specious down-grading of all those elements in the British experience which have been extra-European. The insularity of the British Isles do give their history a special quality. They can also be regarded, from another perspective, as the 'Eastern Atlantic Archipelago' – an outpost of the North American world rather than of the European mainland, or at any rate a crucial bridge between the two worlds. Then again, the demise of the British Empire has also seen substantial immigration into the United Kingdom from some of its former constituent parts, bringing new cultures, languages and religions on a scale which Butterfield could never have conceived in the Second World War. It scarcely needs to be said that this population movement has in turn raised issues concerning 'assimilation', 'integration' and 'multiculturalism' to complicate yet further the question of 'Britishness'. Historians as such have no answer when confronted by these alternatives, though they can speculate in the light of the past. In addition, the emergence of English as *de facto* the world language raises complex problems about the distinctiveness of 'British culture' in a world bombarded by many varieties of English. All of these developments certainly preclude the possibility that 'British history' either can or should simply replace an imperial destiny by a European one as a guiding framework. Yet, when all these provisos have been emphasized, it would appear that it is primarily within Europe that British history will find its future. It is the task of British historians to explain how and why this has come to be so. They should not be too proud to help to explain to a puzzled public the historical roots of this process and the pain and pleasure which still accompanies it.

WILLIAM LAMONT

"That underrated educationist, Mae West, sang her praises of 'A Guy What Takes His Time'. The success of history teaching – at whatever level – rests on that simple truth. "

I HAD JUST GRADUATED with a history degree. I was learning to teach. I faced a class of eleven-year-olds. The subject was Anglo-Saxon England. I decided to tell them about the Witan. The lesson was not going very well, but this particular class was known to be 'pretty dim'. In the middle of my exposition on the structure of the Witan, a child put his hand up. I had learned enough educational theory by then to recognise that there was nothing wholly immoral about such a gesture. 'Well?' I said. 'Please sir, did the Anglo-Saxons wear gloves?' was his query. I was totally disconcerted by the question. There was nothing – in my memory of Bishop Stubbs' *Select Charters* – on this. I blustered: 'Well – yes – er – no. Let's get back to the Witan.' At the end of the class I set a homework on the topic. The general verdict was correct. They were certainly dim. Hardly any had grasped the true nature of the Witan. On the other hand, every one of them began his essay: 'The Anglo-Saxons were a group of people who did not wear gloves.'

This was how I remembered it. But here the historian's caution asserts itself. It happened a long time ago. Isn't it all too neat and contrived an anecdote? All I can say is that I *believe* that I have reported accurately what did take place. Nobody has described that living hell – the transition from graduate to teacher – better than Edward Blishen, in a remarkable series of books. My little experience belongs to Blishen country: to those who have made a similar trek, there will be a flash of recognition; to those who have not, it will seem bizarre and incredible.

Somewhere, in that confrontation of Witan and gloves, we lose many of our young history teachers. Unnerved by the disjunction between what they have learned and what they now have to teach, they flee the teaching profession altogether, or they go on uncomfortably dictating notes about the Witan for the rest of their lives, or (more characteristically) they flee the uncongenial subject, and settle for some subordinate role in a mish-mash interdisciplinary humanities programme, into which the historian can dollop his spoonful of content. But some of us over the past twenty years, painfully, haltingly and with innumerable false starts, have nevertheless come to believe not only that there *is* a correlation between the history taught at School and at University, but that there *has to be* if public investment in the teaching of the subject is to be justified. One woman history don at Oxford not only believed that this was true, but showed – by personal example – how it could be done. I will return to her contribution later in this essay.

For the student teacher, is history any worse than any other subject? Perhaps not, but there are particular expectations imposed on him or her. These expectations take different forms. There are those which derive from the context of the school, in my case for four years, Hackney Downs in north east London. They range from the staff room expectation, that the history teacher will know the answer to the crossword puzzle teaser, to the pupils' expectation that he will not fall below the (immaculate) standards set by his predecessor: 'Mr Williams was good at battles, sir.' Nor – after vainly trying to keep 3B in order – is there respite, in the next period, with 'A' Level history. For there sitting at the back, page open at the relevant section of the Oxford *History of England*, waiting to pounce upon the slightest slip, is the Savonarola of the Sixth (happily, this year translated to a prestigious personal Chair at the University of London). At Hackney Downs, one also had the pressure of parents' expectations. There were those oddly moving Parents' Evenings, where I met the first-generation immigrant parents – hardly able to string an English sentence together – of my voluble, fluent, Cockney pupils. One such parent wasted no time in our encounter. He asked me immediately for the name of the leader of the *first* Russian Revolution. I answered, 'Kerensky'. He replied: 'my boy knows that'. The hopelessness of being a history teacher was encapsulated for me in that exchange. If I'd got it wrong – incredible! *My boy* knows that. If I got it right – so what? My boy knows *that*.

The demands on the young history teacher are imposed as much from outside the school, as from within. The further outside, the shriller those demands. The subject has never wholly liberated itself from Victorian public expectations. Ince's *Outlines of History* was the best-selling history textbook of the nineteenth century, but arguably the philosophy expressed in its preface coloured much of its textbook successors in the twentieth century too: 'if the groundwork be clearly traced in early life, it will scarcely ever be obliterated'. This was the 'structure' metaphor which we see reflected in the very title of Warner and Marten's famous textbook, *The Groundwork of British History*. Its second edition in 1923 contained a 'Chronological Summary of History' as a special insert of blue paper. Its best-selling rival was *The House of History* (Nelson, 1930-2), with its punning four 'Storeys', in place of volumes. It was easier to sustain Ince's metaphor than his confidence in using it. Something clearly was going wrong in the 1920s and 1930s. Children, trained on an unrelieved diet of English chronological history, were patently not very successful in retaining that fundamental groundwork knowledge. Do we detect just a hint of desperation in His Majesty's Inspectors' Report of 1927 – a remarkably frank exposure of the depth of ignorance about history in the schools of the day – with a plea that, nevertheless, there was still value in 'having a few rocks to cling on in a sea of ignorance'? An astonishing de-escalation of aims: from Master Builder to Robinson Crusoe. The drowning sailor clutches at a rock here, a rock there – the Reform Bill, 1832, the Congress of Vienna, 1815 – and hauls himself to safety.

But it wasn't enough. Chronology was on the retreat. New panaceas, however, were at hand. We had M.V.C. Jeffreys, in the mid-1930s, cutting great thematic swathes through chronological history with 'lines of development'.[1] The Second World War predictably advanced the claims for contemporary history. The history teacher, so the argument ran, should have prepared an educated public for the phenomenon of German expansionism; others argued that, for that, we should have gone back to Tacitus.[2] And, after the War, 'World History' was to be the teacher's parish. One of its advocates, Professor Barraclough, coupled this with the demand that the history teacher give up speculating on causes, and concentrate on telling children about results.[3] An interesting decision, which might have cost Professor Cobban, lifelong student of the causes of the French Revolution, his job. That is, until he realised that he could present these same researches under a new title, *Results of the Collapse of the Ancien Regime*. 'People's history' and entrepreneurial history have been more recent attempts to impose coherence on the wayward school syllabus.

What do all these rival schemes have in common? They share an astonishing optimism about the ability of pupils to retain the factual information to prop up these imposing edifices. It is an optimism which does not survive much contact with the classroom. How much history knowledge does the ordinary pupil retain? I think that Neal Ascherson got it about right:

The individual's knowledge of history, to be honest, is a rubbish-tip composed of ill-remembered lessons, what father did in the war, television documentaries with half the instalments missed, bodice-ripper historical novels, fragments of local folklore, the general idea of what that Frenchman seemed to be saying on the train, a dozen feature movies, what we saw of Edinburgh Castle before the wee boy got sick, several jokes about Henry VIII and that oil painting of the king lying dead on the battlefield with his face all green.'[4]

Is this a counsel of despair? No, it's a plea for realism. Accept the limitations – in terms of factual retention – of the average pupil, and then see how the dedicated school teacher begins to work with that unpromising material, transmits some of the enjoyment of the past which he or she already has, begins to inculcate good historical habits, shows how the historian confronts evidence, brings out both the ways in which the past is similar to the present and the ways in which it is different. And, given the right stimulus, what amazing quality of work can be produced by pupils, whose level of *factual* recall may still be pitched at that of Ascherson's description!

In 1971 I asked three students of mine to write down their experiences as beginners in history teaching. I wanted it to be a frank record, warts and all. This became the heart of a volume which I edited,[5] and I think that their essays stand up well, even twenty years on. They gave me what I wanted: not a romance of how-I-tamed-the-class-psychopath, but an honest record of many failures, interspersed with the odd inspiratory success. What shines through is their commitment, to their subject, and to the extraordinarily difficult task of adapting its principles to the needs (at various age and ability levels) of the pupils they were working with. Above all, they gave examples of the written work that their children were producing: it would astonish those University dons, who would be prepared to write off the *creative* capabilities of generations of children, whilst simultaneously overplaying their capacities to *retain* required information.

These three students (one of whom would end up, twenty years later, as a member of the National Curriculum History Working Group) were entering the profession at a time when – it is now often overlooked – history was held in low esteem, the word 'crisis' was being bandied about, and a 1968 survey of the attitudes of 9,677 early school leavers showed history as coming bottom of the poll for interest and enjoyment.[6] The Schools History Project lay in the future, but rereading their essays one can see anticipations of later developments. Young teachers, like these three, would be the catalysts of change, responsive to techniques being developed in the primary schools, ready to expose children at times to selected documents from original sources, collaborating across disciplines with other teachers. This whole process (so caricatured by opponents) has been judiciously evaluated – weaknesses as well as strengths – in the Special Professorial Lecture of John Slater, *The Politics of History Teaching: a humanity dehumanised?*[7]

The frustration in these young teachers' accounts did not come through failure to fulfil some imposing but unrealistic aim set from outside. They never had illusions from the outset about their pupils' capacities to learn a detailed knowledge of the main events of our rough island story. But, for what they *were* trying to do, they badly needed more time. Two periods a week – the usual timetable allowance - was not enough. It is a banal point, and yet those who would impose on the teachers ever more coverage of content (often from laudable motives) ignore it at their peril.

Time was needed for teacher and pupil to develop the relationship that was the prerequisite for further advances. To say that the three beginner-teachers were moving from a subject-centred approach (university) to a pupil-centred approach (school) is a travesty of a complicated process. John Berger captured its essence in his description of the young doctor:

> Previously the sense of mastery which Sassall gained was the result of the skill with which he dealt with emergencies. The possible complications would appear to develop within his own field: they were medical complications. He remained the central character. Now the patient is the central character. He tries to recognise each patient and, having recognised him, he tries to set an example for him – not a morally improving example, but an example wherein the patient can recognise himself.

One of the beginner history teachers recorded his surprise at how, through a chance encounter on the football field, his relationship *in history lessons* was changed with one recalcitrant pupil. It is the point that Berger makes for his young doctor:

> The area in which Sassall practises is one of extreme cultural deprivation, even by British standards. And it was only by working with many of the men of the village and coming to understand something of the techniques that he could qualify for their conversation. They then came to share a language which was a metaphor for the rest of their common experience.[8]

The sharing-a-language takes time. Only by concentrating their syllabus into intensive 'patches' was it possible for the three young teachers to acquire that time. They had a common tool for the job: relevant volumes of Longmans *Then and There* textbooks. This was perhaps the most remarkable textbook revolution of the twentieth century in the teaching of history. The idea was simple, like all great revolutionary ideas. Coverage of content was renounced in theory (it had been given up in practice much earlier). Instead, the aim was to provide clusters of short books around one period in time, which were packed with technical terms (and a glossary at the back), easy to read for primary and junior secondary pupils, but scholarly in the standards required. They arose from the frustration of a woman history don at the pap which children were given in school as medieval history. She determined to change it after her own experience of two years of secondary school teaching, and change it she did.

Marjorie Reeves was her name, and it was through her academic researches that I first encountered her. A.L. Rowse, once reviewing – less than rapturously, it must be said – my book on Richard Baxter, wondered why I was drawn to the study of particularly odious Puritans (a previous book had been on earless William Prynne), when there were so many charming Anglicans around in the seventeenth century (like Clarendon). He comforted himself that Baxter marked some sort of terminus. My next book would, in fact, be on the Prophet Lodowicke Muggleton. So perhaps Rowse was right, and my problems lay in the field of psychopathology. I saw things differently, as of course I would. In studying such men, I was collaborating with other scholars in exposing the millenarian drives in seventeenth-century Puritanism, I would have argued. And no study was more central to that task than Marjorie Reeves's pioneering investigation into the thought of Joachim of Fiore.

Marjorie Reeves's *credo* was unshakeable: 'the problem of teaching is fundamentally the same for the five-year-old as for the twenty-one-year-old'.[9] This did not mean – shades of myself and the Witan – that eleven-year-olds would now digest the writings of Joachim. But she did believe that the mental world of Joachim's age *could* be opened up to the young child, if he or she was not swamped by the demands of content, had time to absorb details (which would be imperfectly measured by his or her factual recall), and had the right sort of textbook as a guide. Her *The Medieval Village*, first of the *Then and There* series, was published in 1954, and these small textbooks have been ever since a run-away commercial and academic success. The series continues today, although the general editorship has passed from Dr Reeves to Dr Fines (who, like her, combines the ability to work with primary schoolchildren and pursue personal scholarly researches – in his case, into Lollardy). Nor should this surprise us. The Sussex University BA Special Subject (two terms of study, documents-based, of a very small period of time: in my case, the English Revolution from 1647 to 1658) is the core of the undergraduate's historical experience; it is blood-brother to the Reeves (and Fines) 'patch' study.

There are siren calls from Right and Left, at the present time, about the direction of school history. It should be about our constitutional history. It should be about the struggle for freedom. It should be based on women's studies. It should be devoted to inter-racialism. The siren calls from either side should be resisted. We have been this way before, with Ince, Warner and Marten, Jeffreys and Barraclough. Their way didn't work, and it won't for their successors. That underrated educationist, Mae West, sang her praises of 'A Guy What Takes his Time'. The success of history teaching – at whatever level – rests on that simple truth. University teachers of history have a softer life than schoolteachers, but they have common aspirations and skills. Both thrive on autonomy: the less interference from the centre the better. I expounded these truisms (or so they seemed then; I would not be quite so confident now) two years ago, when I explained the developments of the past twenty years in teaching history in English schools to over three hundred Chinese school teachers in Tianjin. The idea that the State should keep out of the business of the school curriculum seemed to them absurd. This was pluralism gone mad; the world turned upside down. The first question, at the end of my lecture, came from one uncomprehending Chinese teacher: 'Please, how big is the school textbook in England?' I wanted to reply, but I didn't: 'Historians of the world, unite! You have nothing to lose but your gloves.'

NOTES

1. M.V.C. Jeffreys, 'The Teaching of History by Means of Line of Development', *History*, xxi, 1936, 230-8.
2. G.B. Henderson, 'A Plea for the Study of Contemporary History', *History*, xxvi, 1941, pp 51-5; M. Beloff, 'The Study of Contemporary History', *History*, xxx, 1945, 75-84.
3. G. Barraclough, *History and the Common Man*, Historical Association Pamphlet, 1967, pp 3-15.
4. Neal Ascherson, *Games With Shadows* (London, 1988), p, 12.
5. W. Lamont, ed, *The Realities of Teaching History: Beginnings* (Sussex, 1972).
6. Mary Price, 'History in Danger', *History*, liii, 1968, 342-7.
7. John Slater, *The Politics of History Teaching: a humanity dehumanized?*, Institute of Education Pamphlet, 1988.
8. John Berger, *A Fortunate Man* (Penguin Books, 1969), pp 77, 100.
9. Ann Williams, ed, *Prophecy and Millenarianism* (London, 1980), p 16.

J.C.D. CLARK

"Patriotism is essentially the idea that 'we' are related to 'our' history by something more than contingency: that both the sins and the successes of the fathers are visited upon the children unto the third and fourth generation; that we are part of our past, not tourists."

THE INTELLECTUAL AND cultural underpinnings of present-day national identity are difficult to address directly, especially when (as so often) they involve issues of ethnicity or religion. Instead, public discussion takes place largely on the territory of national history. For decades, academic historical debates in Britain were conducted in the knowledge that they had major consequences in the public arena; but these debates were given sudden focus in 1989 by the need to frame a unified history syllabus for English schools. Our understanding of recent social change, and especially of the significance of the events of the last ten years, had now to be brought to a point.

This challenge came in a context set not only by English domestic politics, but by resurgent Welsh and Scots nationalism, and by the imminent challenge of closer integration into the European Community. Thanks to this context, the three great historical schools which had dominated the nineteenth- and twentieth-century mind – liberal constitutionalism, socialism and imperialism – were now clearly visible as doctrines of state formation at the same moment that we could see that each of them had disintegrated.

First, according to Sir Herbert Butterfield, imperialism – 'the real Tory alternative to the organisation of English history on the basis of the growth of liberty' – had collapsed into liberal constitutionalism during the Second World War.[1] Then, in the 1960s and 1970s, liberal constitutionalism was largely destroyed as an explanatory framework for British politics by the Cambridge school of 'high political' history.[2] Finally, from 1978, socialist historiography was profoundly compromised, partly by econometric economic history, partly by a school of thought provisionally (if unsatisfactorily)

---

* This article first appeared in *History Workshop Journal*, issue 29, Spring 1990.

labelled 'revisionist'.[3] Yet, without these three historical doctrines, we now find that we lack an equally convincing account of exactly who the British are.

Now that the old overarching ideologies have been deconstructed, it seems likely that *all* cultural images will look as if they are regionally and culturally specific. So even Thatcherism, which presents itself as culturally neutral, a formula for prosperity and freedom under law exportable to all European countries, has been *perceived* in Scotland and Wales as an aspect of the cultural imperialism of the South East of England. Similarly, any alternative government which depended on a preponderance of seats in Wales and Scotland is likely now to appear equally partial in England.

Just as Welsh and Scots nationalism are threatening to be the Union's terminal diseases, the old reasons for national unity suddenly look intellectually weak.[4] The three familiar ideologies (liberal constitutionalism, socialism, imperialism) assumed that the problems they addressed were not geographical: each pictured a rivalry of Platonic ideals. However these ideals were received in the constituent parts of the United Kingdom was of marginal relevance.[5] Once we begin to give weight to race and religion, by contrast, it is clear that national identity is distinctly regional within these islands. This state of flux embraces domestic English phenomena also. So insecure are we in our political traditions that when people outside the bourgeois intelligentsia make hesitant efforts to re-appropriate their ethnic national past (the cult of the country house, gentrification, Kenneth Baker's *Faber Book of English History in Verse*) there are howls of protest: history is being 'hijacked' by the Right. Is it?

It would be more accurate to say that two slightly different things were happening: the politicizing of the 'new history' as practised in our schools, and the emergence of a post-modern academic agenda which is beginning to address the world we really live in. The challenge to write a national history syllabus for English schools means that these two things now come into collision.

First, the 'new history'. It is essential to establish that this, too, was post-socialist, post-liberal and post-imperial; those three doctrines stressed objective truth (in different forms) where the 'new history' privileges interpretation. Like capital punishment, it turned into a litmus test of temperament, evoking instinctive sympathy on one side and unbearable irritation on the other. 'Empathy' has become both a synonym for sympathy (let's side with the underdogs rather than argue to defend our intuition that they are indeed exploited) and a euphemism for guessing (can you teach mathematics by empathy? or German?). History in depth, 'patch history', celebrates history 'from below', but has been accused of locking children from poor backgrounds into the similar experiences of their impoverished ancestors, an eventless round of material deprivation, limited intellectual horizons and unsuccessful resentments.

History's methodological diversity is an ancient theme, and the diversity shows every sign of increasing still further. Underlying it is the old rivalry between state and society: which shall we emphasise? Although this choice is sometimes politicized, it need not be: clearly, some social history is conservative in its implications (Peter Laslett, Alan Macfarlane); some political history is equally radical (Kenneth Morgan, Ben Pimlott). Similarly with the choice between depth and breadth: E.P. Thompson and Sir Lewis Namier, who wrote detailed studies of narrow time-spans, can be aligned against the broad sweeps of Christopher Hill and Sir Geoffrey Elton. Cutting across these issues, however, is a different and loaded one with which the others might be confused. The most sensitive choice is between studies within the public arena (power politics, social and foreign policy, political and economic thought) and studies of the sub-groups (communities, sects, trade unions) which might be analysed as resisters of the claims of central authority, and of the idea of national identity which it sustains. Grassroots history (or the history of gender, or that of ethnic groups) can never give such a sense of national identity or national pride. Nations are defined by what their populations as a whole have done in the public arena, and that is a story of heroism (or cowardice), nobility (or ignominy), idealism (or duplicity) rather than of localist introversion.[6]

From the vantage point of King's College, Cambridge, Gareth Stedman Jones has called[7] for a return to wide horizons and a clear narrative backbone to national history. So, from a different point on the political spectrum, has Robert Skidelsky in a rival syllabus to that of the official Working Group, led by Michael Saunders Watson.[8] These objections may be elitist, but hardly seem inherently of 'the Right'. They may be simply functional: the 'new history' is likely to disillusion anyone (like admissions tutors) who has to take the subject seriously and clear up the mess. But, of course, there was a serious purpose behind it. Certain groups clearly sought to use the new *methods* as an excuse for marginalising the old *contents* of which they disapproved – the story of power, liberty, wealth creation, religion, empire. The emphasis on teaching skills rather than knowledge could be used as a stalking-horse. The demand to empathise was, as it turned out, a way of weighting minorities rather than the majority culture. The 'new history' was really the world view of the plural society rather than of a socialist society: Attlee would have dismissed it with contempt.

Second, the post-modern academic agenda. Apparently independent of political polemics, issues rise and fall in the historical pop charts. Twenty years ago it was all Levellers, John Wilkes, industrial take-off, Luddites, Reform Bills, the long march of Everyman. Now the hit tunes are religion, demographic discipline, state formation, national identity, a strong bureaucracy, a resilient ruling elite.[9] Not all of this should be credited to one politician, not even Mrs Thatcher. The heritage industry in some ways contradicts her modernism: the proliferation of visitable country houses was a measure of the passing of patrician culture; in the last decade, those artificially preserved mines, mills, factories and docks have echoed the disappearance of an old industrial base. This too would have happened whatever party was in office.

If popular history is still locked in the old stereotypical traps, post-modern academic history since the late 1970s has broken free from more and more of them. Increasingly, it is a study of survivals rather than origins, long continuities rather than revolutionary transformations. No fashionable agenda is ever fully translated into the school syllabus, which tends to stick to the complacent Whiggism of 'Our Island Story'. But the post-modern academic agenda has inexorably come to offer an effective challenge to the 'new history', and now clamours for its dethronement.

Political problems arise because history is more than just a set of techniques – scepticism, impartiality, investigation, weighing evidence. Not much of these can be effectively done in schools in any case. The controversy explodes because school history especially is, in addition to its techniques, an initiation into a culture by the transmission of a heritage. The role of university history may be deconstruction; but popular (and school) history will always have an element of celebration. The question really is: what shall we celebrate? It is hard enough to dissuade academics from doing this;[10] to dissuade popular historians, seemingly impossible. So popular history remains a battlefield in a contest for cultural hegemony.

The argument therefore turns not on whether history should be patriotic (only a handful of austere positivist historians seem to argue that it should be neutral) but on what form the patriotism should take: should it be a story of achievement, advance, enlightenment? Or should it emphasise a dark side – exploitation, suffering, poverty? Nothing in the *methods* of scholarship can answer this question: it is essentially political. But post-modern historiography has made a profound (and still only partially appreciated) difference to the terms in which this problem is phrased, by explaining historically many of the categories whose unchallengeable validity in fact begged many questions, like 'revolution', 'democracy' and 'class'.

The History Working Group was given perfunctory guidance on the nature of an acceptable syllabus: 'The study of history in schools should help pupils to understand how a free and democratic society developed over the centuries'.[11] Any society can be expected to demand that publicly-funded education will embody and endorse its values; yet how are we to characterise those values? Does the sentence quoted stand as a platitude, unworthy of emphasis, or does it epitomise a distinct and potent set of ideas? On one side can be found complaints that history is being hi-jacked by Thatcherism; on the other, the perception that the Thatcherite experiment has so far espoused no new historical vision but merely re-emphasised a picture of broadening parliamentary democracy and the rule of law last championed by academic historians in the 1930s. Yet this old story would not have been wheeled out again if it did not have *some* new relevance: as now used, it is a powerful negation of pluralism.

The malaise addressed by the idea of a standardised national syllabus is a plural society, not a socialist society. And here the school of 'high political' history has its relevance, since – as Richard Brent observes[12] – its essential purpose was not to privilege ambition and manoeuvre in politics over policy and principle, but both to deflate liberal high-mindedness and to discard socialist reductionism, and so to remove a certain teleology from British historiography (a teleology which predicted, in effect, that the Thatcherite counter-revolution against pluralism *could not happen*). The 'high political' school of historians had shared an insight into human imperfectibility which distinguished them from liberals and socialists alike and gave a point of contact with the moral vision at the heart of Thatcherite politics since 1979.

When Conservative politicians appealed to a constitutionalist tradition, therefore, it was to a tradition profoundly modified by a recent academic critique. Formal constitutional arrangements no longer had a peculiar sanctity, and successive ministries since 1979 were unusually willing to abolish or transform the institutions of government. Kenneth Baker, Sir Keith Joseph and Margaret Thatcher still emphasised, as themes in their historical vision, the rule of law and the development of democracy. For a government confident in its democratic mandate, and using the law to defend the individual against corporatism, this was not unreasonable. Certainly, political historians had done nothing to breathe life into these old themes: from Geoffrey Elton and Conrad Russell to John Vincent, Andrew Jones, Michael Bentley and Robert Skidelsky, the whole force of academic opinion had been sceptical of the motives of parliamentarians, the effectiveness of the Commons, and the democratic integrity of its election. But the government's attitudes have much deeper academic roots in, for example, Alan Macfarlane's reassertion of a medieval 'enterprise culture' against the Marxist historians' picture of a collectivist peasant society, in Conrad Russell's and other scholars' demolition of the Marxist model of the English civil war, and in Tony Wrigley's and Roger Schofield's demonstration of Malthusian disciplines underpinning eighteenth-century economic advance.[13] These themes have yet to reach the textbooks: there is no explicitly Thatcherite history in the sense that there was a liberal and then a Marxist history.

If the debate can indeed be shifted back to 'Our Island Story', however, the Right is on defensible ground. The historiography of the rule of law and the broadening of democracy is not easily seen through, certainly at school level; and its antithesis – a negative history of the oppression of minorities – has yet to find its Macaulay, let alone its Erskine May, its Bagehot or its Dicey. 'Women's history' and 'black studies' carried to a *reductio ad absurdum* the exclusiveness of the old (white, male) tradition of 'labour history'. The failure of these new varieties over more than a decade to generate a real alternative vision, a grand narrative, is now clear; despite its wide currency, the 'new history' has essentially failed in its wider political purpose. It has merely debilitated those who profess and practise it. But this happy picture seems more likely to be upset by the unexpected – by those forces like provincial nationalism and religious commitment which were politely omitted from the world view of the Whig G.M. Trevelyan and the Socialist G.D.H. Cole alike.

Given how much of our history has been rewritten in the last ten years, and how much has changed in politics under Mrs Thatcher, it is peculiar how *few* of these issues the alternative syllabus proposed by Professor Skidelsky addressed. Its end-point was clearly *not* radical individualism, entrepreneurial zeal, family values, public order. It spoke of parliamentary democracy, cabinet government and the rule of law ('Our Island Story'), but only to identify a British heritage as we merge into the EEC. These things, thanks to the post-modern academic agenda, can now be taken for granted (at least by scholars). What his syllabus seemed to stress was the one issue of which academic historians have still, so far, fought shy: the diverse ethnic composition of the population of these islands.

It is not a Thatcherite property-owning democracy which seems to stand at the end of Skidelsky's implied teleology, but moral and cultural pluralism. It is a society in racial turmoil, a society which has still not come to terms with massive immigration for the unspoken reason that it still lacks an historical understanding of how and why it happened. It seems likely that it is a story which could not be told without discrediting Britain's claims to be a democratic state, just as the observed facts of ethnic diversity clearly override the imperatives of socialism at constituency level, and put into reverse the assumptions of imperialism.

The initial reaction of the Skidelsky syllabus seems to be a rather doubtful one if it is placing the West Indians, Asians (and Hong Kong Chinese?) in the same category as the Scots, Irish and Welsh. Is England's dominance of her 'Celtic' neighbours really a good context for understanding her relations with her new citizens? The Scots, Irish and Welsh have ancient histories within these islands. But how far have new immigrant groups sought to integrate themselves into British history, to appropriate it, to become its heirs? How far have we sought to teach it to them? Is this approach to acculturation anything more than the tub-thumping characterised as 'tell-the-children-how-Wolfe-won-Quebec'? These questions were ignored for two decades; now the answers become steadily less self-evident.

It is legitimate to address what Sir Keith Joseph called 'the development of the shared values which are a distinctive feature of British society and culture and which continue to shape private attitudes and public policy'. This is a realistic goal whether taught by the 'new' methods or the 'old'. But in addition to this, voices as diverse as Gareth Stedman Jones and the new Minister of Education, John MacGregor, have called for more British history on a chronological framework. Does this have an inbuilt bias to the Right? It is hard to see why it should. A national history which takes account of England's chequered relations with Scotland, Ireland and Wales is unlikely to encourage complacency about the neutral wisdom of England's ruling ethic. But it does focus on patriotism.

Patriotic history is not a series of sentimental anecdotes of Drake, Nelson or the Battle of Britain, though these images can still evoke it. Patriotism is essentially the idea that 'we' are related to 'our' history by something more than contingency; that both the sins and the successes of the fathers are visited upon the children unto the third and fourth generation; that we are part of our past, inhabitants not tourists. To a remarkable extent, this assumption is shared by Left and Right, but different conclusions drawn: one side wants us to shoulder the moral burden of eighteenth-century slavery, the other invites us to take credit for nineteenth-century democracy and the rule of law. One praises the legacy of the Levellers, the other hails the heritage of Robert Adam and Capability Brown. Both the dark and light sides are 'ours'; we disagree on which to stress. Patriotism is alive and well as long as such arguments go on. If so, it is unperceptive to dismiss the Left as unpatriotic or the Right as jingoistic. They both care. The problem really comes when the formula has to be amended to include those who are not British by lineage, inheritance or bequest.

The idea that there was some period in the past when 'we' were more like 'ourselves', more authentically English (or Welsh, or Scots, or Irish) is an ancient one and shared equally by most parties. It is usually equally bogus; but there are periods of profound change when it has a larger element of truth, and when it unites (traditionalist) Left and Right against the (rationalist) 'centre'. Recent decades constitute one such time.

How do we respond? The pluralist replies by emphasising the unassimilated roles of Welsh, Irish and Scots in past centuries; the conservative stresses the way in which our nation state was assembled and (largely) held together despite these centrifugal forces. Neither seems yet to have taken on board the immense power of religion in fuelling lasting sectional hatreds. The new agenda is still evolving, and Salman Rushdie may yet write an unhappy paragraph.

Has the old vision (nation state, parliamentary democracy, empire) been undercut by new methods emphasising the relativity of knowledge and the priority of interpretation? If no interpretation can claim universal validity, then no subject matter can be privileged. True, so far. But this just leaves rival interpretations legitimately competing for ascendancy, or, to borrow Gramsci's concept, hegemony. If all knowledge is relative, then why not teach children the perspective on the past that 'we' value most? Indeed, can 'we' avoid doing this? It takes militant Muslim communities among us to show us, by contrast, that that is what is happening, and that it is inevitable that it should happen.

We cannot expect to arrive at an agreed, neutral version of our national past, disinfected, tasteless and unutterably safe, fit to be taught uncontroversially to captive school audiences like a 'dead' language. British history has never been like that, and we have no reason to expect that it ever will be, whoever (educationalist, historian or politician) writes the syllabus. The idea that 'the Right' is doing something new (and therefore in itself illegitimate) in projecting a vision of British history is itself bad history: historiography has always been 'essentially contested' from Shakespeare's history plays through Clarendon and Macaulay to Hill and Hobsbawm.[14] If there *is* a history from the Right, it must stand or fall by its scholarly force. Liberal constitutionalism, socialism and imperialism were all historiographical doctrines resting on claims to objective knowledge; with their passing, the determinants of national identity no longer operate in obvious and reductionist ways. We are not automatically conscious of race or religion or regional loyalty. We see instead a variety of regional and ethnic cultural ideals seeking hegemony; but hegemony is a game in which all can join.

NOTES

1. 'This epic of British expansion has been swallowed into the original system of the whigs': Herbert Butterfield, *The Englishman and His History,* Cambridge, 1944, pp 81-2.

2. Cf Michael Bentley, 'What is Political History?', *The Durham University Journal*, 70, 1978, 133-9; Richard Brent,'Butterfield's Tories: "High Politics" and the Writing of Modern British Political History', *Historical Journal*, 30, 1987, 943-54. So complete was the success of this critique that (i) it has effectively ceased, and (ii) research into nineteenth- and twentieth-century political history in any other idiom is still substantially inhibited.

3. The term derives from the scholarship of early-Stuart England. For a review of its implications, cf J.C.D. Clark, *Revolution and Rebellion: State and Society in England in the Seventeenth and Eighteenth Centuries,* Cambridge, 1986.

4. These themes are further explored in the present author's 'The History of Britain: A Composite State in a *Europe des Patries?*' in J.C.D. Clark (ed), *Ideas and Politics in Modern Britain*, London, 1990, pp 32-49.

5. Before the dominance of these three ideologies, but especially socialism, textbooks of British history often devoted *more* space to Scotland, Ireland and Wales than they were to do in the twentieth century: cf Raphael Samuel, 'In Search of Britain', *New Statesman & Society*, 25 August 1989, 21-4.

6. 'A balkanised left, unable to tell a story of Britain at all because it disputes the existence of a character called Britain, has found it very hard to counter the Thatcherite version': Sarah Benton, 'National Anthems', *New Statesman & Society*, 9 June 1989, 22.

7. At a conference held at Ruskin College, Oxford, on 3 June 1989.

8. Robert Skidelsky and others, 'G.C.S.E. History: An Alternative Approach' (24 May 1989); Michael Saunders Watson and others, 'National Curriculum History Working Group: Interim Report' (10 August 1989).

9. For the way in which methodological changes re-illuminate certain aspects of our past see – for one issue – J.C.D. Clark, 'On Moving the Middle Ground: The Significance of Jacobitism in Historical Studies' in Eveline Cruickshanks and Jeremy Black (eds), *The Jacobite Challenge*, Edinburgh, 1988, pp 177-88.

10. The tercentenary celebrations of the Glorious Revolution revealed the peculiar residual strength of the desire among academic historians to declare that event a Good Thing and to disparage those of their colleagues who sought to present a balanced picture, especially of the bloodshed in Scotland and Ireland.

11. This doctrine was, presumably, thought to be 'consistent with Sections 44 and 45 of the Education (No 2) Act 1986 which prohibits

political indoctrination and requires balanced presentation of opposing views': 'National Curriculum History Working Group, Interim Report', Appendix 2, p 105.

12. Brent, 'Butterfield's Tories' (see note 2).

13. Alan Macfarlane, *The Origins of English Individualism*, Oxford, 1978, and *The Culture of Capitalism*, Oxford, 1987; E.A. Wrigley and R.S. Schofield, *The Population History of England 1541-1871*, London, 1981.

14. Cf Sir Herbert Butterfield, *The Englishman and his History*, and *George III and the Historians,* London, 1957; J.G.A. Pocock, *The Ancient Constitution and the Feudal Law*, 2nd edn, Cambridge, 1987.

CONRAD RUSSELL

"Moreover, since historians tend to hold their convictions with passion, and, as they believe, with conscience, any attempt to preserve a national mythology is bound to fail for the same reason that religious persecution failed: it is too labour-intensive a process to be viable for very long."

ONE OF OUR leading historians, when coming into work on a commuter train to King's Cross, was once drawn into conversation by a banker, who asked him how he could justify spending so much of his life on the study of things which are dead and gone. Finally, after a long series of exchanges, he fell back on the reply: 'because there's a market for it'. This reply reduced the banker to silence.

Anyone looking at the annual statistics for visitors to the Tower of London, at the crowds of genealogists in local record offices, or at the success of historical programmes on television, must be inclined to concede that this argument contains truth. The desire to know one's own past, like the desire to know who one's parents are, does appear to represent a deep psychological need. Just as most people feel a need for ancestry, so most countries feel a need for national mythology, and those who are most poorly supplied with it put the greatest effort into constructing it. The creation of a national mythology, as Czech admiration for Comenius may illustrate, may be a potent force in the politics of the present day. For that reason, the content of historical teaching is always likely to be intensely interesting to politicians, and their interest tends to substantiate Hobbes's proposition that 'the end of knowledge therefore is power'.

It is here that it is possible to claim, as Professor Elton has done, a connection between the study of academic history and liberty, for the central claim of academic history is that it tries to ensure that mythologies should be true. Since historians are men and women who need mythologies as much as the rest of us, their attempts in this direction must always be imperfect. Fortunately, however, we are a contentious lot, and our errors and misinterpretations always risk being checked by the scrutiny of our peers. That we arrive at truth by such rough and ready methods is more than most of us would claim, but at least perhaps we succeed in sometimes reducing the area of error.

One of the most complex and confusing themes in historiographical change is the link between changing academic understanding and changing national mythologies. This is the classic problem of chicken and egg. Do national mythologies change because historians have discovered, on empirical grounds, that they are false? Or do historians discover new things in response to the changing demands made upon them by the public? The antithesis between fashion and truth is not, of course, absolute: in cases where historians ask new questions, they may on occasion discover new things whose truth is indubitable, simply because they are the first to go to the sources and ask. If the historian responds to the demands of his or her public, this does not prove that their new findings are false. On the other hand, it does not prove that they are true, though it may make them welcome.

The process is perhaps best understood as circular, or at least spiral. Whether the spiral is seen as upward or downward will, of course, in each case be a matter of opinion: there is no need to invoke a Victorian faith in 'progress' to justify historiographical change: like birth and death, it is simply one of the facts of human existence. Any attempt to bring it to an end will inevitably fail, both because it would involve teaching manifest untruths, and because it would not satisfy its market. A view of the Reformation which did not look beyond the horizons of *Foxe's Book of Martyres* for example, might satisfy the Reverend Ian Paisley, but for that very reason, it would fail to satisfy many others. Moreover, since historians tend to hold their convictions with passion, and, as they believe, with conscience, any attempt to preserve a national mythology is bound to fail for the same reasons that religious persecution failed: the suppression of conscience is far too labour-intensive a process to be viable for very long.

All this is relevant to any attempt to assess why and for what ends history ought to be taught in schools. It helps to explain why it is not possible to do as Sheila Lawlor of the Centre for Policy Studies asks, and decide 'what it is that pupils ought to know on leaving school'. That is an attempt to buck the intellectual market. Anyone who thinks it is possible to draw up a list of 'what every schoolboy knows' should ask how many of us know what was on Macaulay's original list of 'what every schoolboy knows'. It was who killed Montezuma, and who strangled Atahualpa. These facts, so far as I know, have not been shown to be false, but I would be very surprised indeed if one per cent of schoolboys or schoolgirls know them now, and any attempt to include them in the attainment targets for the National Curriculum would surely be dismissed as bizarre. If we should attempt today to list a series of facts to be included in attainment targets, we would surely find, with the more rapid pace of historical research, that we would not have to wait 170 years for them to be regarded as bizarre.

Indeed, thanks to the alertness of our national press, and the speed of the fax machine, we would be unlikely to have to wait as much as 170 hours. Professor Norman Stone, writing in the *Sunday Times* on 8 April 1990, conceded that 'historians and the general public might disagree as to the interpretation of our national history', but insisted that 'there are certain fundamentals upon which we need to agree'. This sounds distressingly like the argument of those who were dismayed by religious division in the seventeenth century that we should and could agree on 'fundamentals'. John Hales, a Fellow of Eton in the 1630s, was asked what he meant by 'fundamentals', and replied: 'those things on which all men can agree'. He and many of his contemporaries began such a list with the doctrine of the Trinity, a claim which was almost immediately followed by the rise of Socinianism and Unitarianism. If Professor Stone were to expose his list of 'fundamentals' to the scrutiny of his fellow-historians, he would be unlikely to fare much better. This is not just a matter of changing historical fashion. In my own period of study, a considerable number of the basic 'facts' we all knew when I was an undergraduate are now known to be demonstrably false. Henry VII, when he died, did not leave an immense treasure: this was a myth put about by Henry VII himself, and his own accounts do not sustain it. The Act in Restraint of Appeals of 1533 did not, as 'every schoolboy knew' when I was one myself, sever all links between England and Rome: it continued to allow, for example, appeals in cases of heresy. The Commons in 1604 did not 'pass' the Apology of the Commons: they referred it back to committee for re-drafting. The Parliamentary appropriation of supply in 1624 was not the result of a constitutionally aggressive Commons pressing to limit the royal prerogative: it was a compromise between the King and his favourite the Duke of Buckingham, forced through Parliament by the Lord Treasurer and the Chancellor of the Exchequer. Any of these things might well have been included in a list of 'facts' put into a hypothetical attainment target thirty years ago, and their presence there now would be an intolerable requirement to teach error by law. We have no idea which of the 'facts' we might insert in attainment targets now will be shown to be false in the next thirty years, but we can be sure that some of them will. A requirement to teach specific 'facts' cannot be compatible with the duty of the teacher to teach truth as he or she sees it.

To say children need to learn facts is perfectly acceptable, and to say they need chronology is perfectly acceptable. Chronology is one of the basic tools of the historian, and it should be one of the central points of historical method not to answer the question 'why' until we can answer the question 'when'. That programmes of study should give an indication, not couched in any inflexible form, of the sort of factual knowledge which may be expected, is necessary guidance. Shifting facts into the attainment targets would move the facts from the discretionary guidance into the more mandatory area of directions. The vital distinction is between saying children need to know facts, which the History Working Group does say, and saying they need particular facts, which it does not say, and which only infallible authority could say.

This approach makes it possible to get away from the sterile argument of the past twenty years between skills and knowledge. It is hard to see how either can well exist without the other. The question 'what is knowledge' is one demanding quite exceptional skill. It is not, of course, suggested that our younger schoolchildren should constantly have their noses rubbed in such complex questions, yet in any school which does not replace all its books every five years, some points in the books will be known to the teacher to be false, and a teacher who tells his or her pupils that the information in the book is false owes them some explanation of how we know it is false. Knowledge demands skills, but equally, skills demand knowledge. The most important historical skill is that of putting information into context, and the selection of the right context is one which demands very considerable knowledge. The History Working Group seems to have given us the chance to leave the argument about skills versus knowledge behind us, and go on to next business.

It should follow from what has been said already that there can be no objectively right list of things about which schoolchildren should be taught. Any list of programmes of study *must* include an element of the arbitrary, and one person's list of the arbitrary will be very different from another's. It must follow, then, that no one can expect to be totally and entirely satisfied by the list of subjects included in programmes of study. The most important point here is that they must be subject to regular revision. Over a fairly short period, probably five or ten years, they will cease to match either current knowledge or current interests. The majority of these programmes of study may be good for twenty years, but if the whole list is left unchanged for that long, it will include some which command no interest, and exclude some others for which there is a large demand. Unless there is an *automatic* procedure for them to be reviewed, pressure for a review will risk repeating, every few years, the sort of political controversy which is going on at the moment, to the detriment of the whole curriculum.

My own judgement of the inclusions and exclusions in the programmes of study, then, is as arbitrary as anyone else's. When this is said, and granted that this is not identical to the list I would have chosen myself, I think it is as good as can be expected. In particular, the Report is to be warmly praised for refusing to join the battle between political and social history. This should be regarded, in the words of the Godfrey Davis car hire advertisement, as 'the most idiotic competition in Britain'. Both happened to the same people at the same times, and it is hard to see how either can ever be properly understood without some knowledge of the other. The Report's 'PESC' formula, whereby the political, economic, social and cultural aspects of any period must all be studied, should eliminate the worst excesses on both sides of the argument, while permitting teachers to do what they will inevitably do anyway, which is putting the strongest emphasis on the side they are most comfortable with. This sort of linkage will do something to protect the subject at later stages against the worst sorts of specialized fission. If I find, as I sometimes do, information about children being given sticky cakes to eat during journeys, I will not need, to put the information in context, to consult separately with a historian of childhood and a historian of transport, because neither can consider both sides of the information. Here, the National Curriculum will provide a base which will be vital to the preservation of history as a single subject, which in the United States has sometimes appeared to be in doubt. It should also serve to limit the tendency to fission inherent in course-unit degrees.

A good history curriculum should include a solid helping of history of the country the children live in, no matter which country this may be. This is partly in order to enable them to understand the country they live in, and partly because a coherent curriculum should include one element which enables people to follow a theme across a long period of time. At the same time, it is not possible to understand our own country, any more than it is to understand anything else, without seeing it in context. This implies some knowledge of European culture. It is unlikely that any medieval historian will dispute that the Catholic Christendom of the middle ages has provided a common intellectual heritage to the countries which belonged to it. It is only in the light of some such knowledge that we can even think about the different uses of this heritage in, for example, Spain and Scotland. At the same time, it is impossible to understand any civilization without a comparative dimension, and this creates a strong case for a knowledge of at least one civilization outside the confines of western Europe. Granted that it is impossible to do everything (something not all critics seem to remember), the Report has done as well in aiming at this sort of balance as could be expected.

Within this collection of programmes, I am perhaps best placed to comment on what I know most about, which is British history. Here, the Report has produced proposals which break new ground, and are to be warmly welcomed. When they talk about British history, they do not merely mean the history of greater England, as illustrated in the textbook which once described how, under Henry VIII, 'Britain declared war on Scotland'. The authors understand that the historic Britain, even if not the present-day Britain, included four nations, the English, the Welsh, the Scots and the Irish. Even if the Irish may claim to be excluded from any list of the present-day British, they certainly have to be included in any historic study of Britain. The authors of the Report understand, and have been fortified in their understanding by the Working Group on the National Curriculum for Wales, that the history of Britain consists both of these four separate national histories and of the interaction between them. The Declaration of Arbroath of 1320 with its claim that Scotland was 'a nation rightly struggling to be free', and its insistence that 'while there are a hundred of us left alive, we will never submit to England', thus acquires a claim to inclusion in the latest list of 'what every schoolboy knows'.

Such a claim is justifiable, among many other reasons, because even the internal history of England cannot be understood without it. At the Union of the Crowns in 1603, the Scots did not rescind the Declaration of Arbroath, for, as they saw it, they had not submitted to England: their king had inherited England, which had submitted to him. The Scots' perception of what had happened in 1603 was that it was a union of the crowns of two free and independent sovereign states, without prejudice to the national sovereignty of either. This perception created an opportunity for copycat emulation by the Irish, and a perpetual pitfall for the English, who tended to ignore the fact that any such thing had happened. It was the mere fact that the English ignored this event which made it create so many unexpected problems for them.

One of the most fascinating themes in the history of Britain, especially between 1603 and the Act of Union with Scotland in 1707, is the difficulties of running a state which was a supra-national institution. Few things in the national history of England have caused us more difficulty than understanding our Civil War, and it is a difficulty we share with those who lived through it. The difficulty has been because we (and they) have failed to understand it in the British context in which it happened. The English Civil War was the fourth round in a series of some ten British internal wars stretching from 1639 to 1651, and including, for the first time since the fourteenth century, four Scottish invasions of England in the space of thirteen years. It is surely not stretching credulity to argue that an underlying instability in the relations between England and Scotland was among the causes of these events. In fact, the English Civil War was a temporary distraction from the underlying struggle, which was for English supremacy in the British Isles. It was only because Charles I pursued this aim in a cause so unpopular that some half his English subjects came to prefer the Scots to him, that the Scots were able to call on the English Parliament as allies against him. They proved, in Christopher Thorne's phrase, 'allies of a kind', and ultimately more successful in asserting English superiority over Scotland than Charles had ever been. The History Working Group's case for treating the history of Britain as genuinely British need not depend on any presumed political utility in doing so: it rests on the fact that this approach may, for the first time ever, enable the English to see their own history sufficiently in context to be able to understand it.

Here, of course, the Group are asking for something formidably ambitious. Because they have, for once, brought proposals for school history up to date with the cutting edge of research, they are asking for something for which books suitable for school use are not yet written. Getting them written in time for use will be a challenge to historians and to publishers, but one to which they are capable of rising. What is more doubtful is whether school budgets are capable of rising to this challenge. The Educational Publishers' Council have estimated the cost of books for the National Curriculum in History at £58 million, and this figure may be an underestimate, for they may well not have allowed for the difficulty of teaching genuinely British history with English history textbooks. If the requirement is introduced without the means to make it achievable, demoralization will be the only result. The effect of teaching schoolchildren that requirements need not be met is unedifying, and not conducive to good citizenship. If the funds are not available to do the job properly, the introduction of the National Curriculum must be postponed until they are.

JANET L. NELSON

"Christian beliefs and practices were shared (and sometimes argued over) throughout Europe, East as well as West . . . and the teaching of medieval history cannot be other than resolutely European . . . to teach medieval history as national history is an anachronism: to teach one bit of medieval Europe apart from the other is a contradiction in terms. "

THE HISTORY OF the Middle Ages figures at extreme ends of the educational system but not in the middle. It is taught, on the one hand, in the older-established universities, often chosen as a specialism by the ablest and most committed students. It is taught, on the other hand, in primary schools, on the reasonable assumption that knowledge of the past should 'begin at the beginning', and in the well-founded belief that it offers a special stimulus to the imaginations of the young: kings and queens inhabit a world of pageantry, colour and romance which easily shades into myth. That assumption, and that belief, underlie the History Working Group's prescriptions for the teaching of medieval history: they recommend quite a lot for children up to the age of eleven, then a single course on medieval British history for eleven-twelve year-olds, along with another optional course also on medieval British history for the eleven-fourteen age-group (Key Stage 3).[1] (In England, on past form, as the Working Group ruefully recognises, 'British' will generally mean 'English'.) Under these proposals, what has hitherto been a widespread tendency to leave medieval history 'behind' at fifteen-sixteen year-old level becomes a requirement. No GCSE course in medieval history exists at present: adoption of the Working Group's proposals would mean that it never will. A dwindling number of schools, few if any of them in the state sector, offer medieval history at A-level: again, it seems likely that the implementation in the near future of a new sixteen-eighteen year-old curriculum will see off medieval history there too. In short most school leavers are left with the strong impression that only twentieth-century history is relevant and worth the attention of young adults. The vast majority of A-level candidates, hence new undergraduates in history departments, will have done modern history and nothing but since the age of twelve.

This categorising, and relegation, and rendering invisible, of medieval history needs to be challenged. It is neither a 'hard' subject, nor an 'easy' one. It has no one particular audience: it is not best suited for teaching to the *crème de la crème*, any more than it is specially attractive for small children. It is a subject that offers intellectual as well as imaginative stimulus to students of every age: the small child's fascination with kings and queens, and the scholarly study of royal courts, patronage, government, belong on the same continuum. Medieval history can appropriately be taught at every level – including GCSE and A-level; and it needs that 'middle', if its earlier stages are to be taken seriously and its top-growth is not to be stunted. At universities where it is an available option, most history students choose to take at least one medieval paper. Medieval history clearly has wide appeal: it needs no protected or privileged status in the curriculum. But it deserves just as much prominence as other fields. It offers – no more than other periods of history, but also no less – knowledge, and awareness, of specific and useful kinds. Recent events, products as they are of the medieval as well as of the more recent past, and of long-run as well as short-run continuity and change, demonstrate the relevance of medieval history to an understanding of the world we live in. Medieval history gives no unique access to moral virtue (any more than any other kind of history does) in terms of insight, tolerance, rapport. But it is particularly well-suited to teaching what the Working Group terms 'the distinctive methodology' whereby historians 'attempt to construct their own coherent accounts of the past by the rigorous testing of evidence which is often incomplete'.[2]

The heart of the subject, at school as at university, will no doubt remain political history, taking 'political' in the widest sense, to include – along with the structures – the sociology and ideology of power. Teaching should cover, not just institutions and government, but the individuals and groups who used, participated in, and exploited power as well as those who were its victims, and those who were both exploiters and victims; and also the ideas and perceptions of power held in the minds of all these. Political history has to be concerned with chronology; but it need not be confined to 'events' in the narrow sense, nor should interpretations be teleological, that is, working back from known outcomes to deduce a chain of causation. The first rule of history-teaching is never to assume that change proceeded on straight lines. The second rule involves the exercise of imagination: think yourself back into the time of your historical subjects – who did not know (as we know) what came next. As a British prime minister once said, a week is a long time in politics. Human decisions are never wholly predictable, and their outcomes still less so. Might-have-beens are always worth contemplating. To reconstruct them, however, demands careful assessment of all available evidence – including 'submerged layers' which are often peculiarly difficult to recover: history is generally written by victors, not vanquished, and for the medieval period, it is often only the victors who have left direct evidence.

The third rule of history-teaching is that perceptions vary with the beholder. It is not just historians whose interpretations differ. People in the past had different effects on, and were affected differently by, the situations and events they experienced. Political history thus includes contestation and subversion along with legitimation, rejection along with accommodation, programmes of community as well as hierarchy, and alternative visions of well-being, opposed images of order; images of women as powerless but also power-filled – like the medieval Virgin Mary depicted sometimes as a peasant-girl, sometimes as queen, or images of children as passive victims but also as ideals of pure active power – like the Infant Jesus or the child-saint before whom adults kneel.

The medieval image most often encountered in text-books is 'the feudal pyramid'. It is not wholly anachronistic, for something like it was in some medieval minds. But it is monochrome and static: hence, misrepresents the diversity and change of a millennium's experiences. In practice medieval monarchs derived such powers as they had from interactions with various communities.[3] Rulers needed consensus, for the means of coercion at their disposal were weak and intermittent. Provincials, from aristocrats to peasants, contested the tax-demands of central governments; and tensions within royal families meant that a prince could usually be found to act as a figurehead for revolt. Courtiers in France and England publicised the anointed king's miraculous powers to heal scrofula, yet in both kingdoms, royal saints were held up to their successors by rebellious subjects as models of justice. In Aragon, nobles reputedly swore to be loyal to their king on condition that he respected their privileges – 'and if not, not'. Though kingship was the norm (and biblically-inspired), it was also criticised (and the Bible's account of the origins of kingship in Israel had God forewarning of the abuses of power). Alternative regimes were conceivable (and likewise biblically-authorised) – the patriarchal household of Abraham, for instance. City-republics in Italy claimed sovereign power by invoking the Virgin Mary as their sole governor.

In these medieval contrasts and oppositions, the Christian religion and the Christian Church played a historically-crucial part in events, structures, perceptions, arguments – and also in the media (from sermons to architecture and ritual) through which knowledge about all those was purveyed. Churchmen publicised good rulers, but also bad ones who were criticised and repented, like the Old Testament David. Both Alfred the cake-burner and Canute the non-ruler of the waves were models of royal humility. Ecclesiastical history was a fertile source of contestation: martyr-saints against tyrannical emperors; Becket against Henry II. Such images legitimised resistance.

Because of the Church's two-fold vision – of community as well as hierarchy – and its ambiguous relationship to secular power – often supportive, yet sometimes hostile – the perspective of any student of the Middle Ages has to be bi-focal: on disruption as well as on continuity; on hierarchy and stability and legitimation, yes; but also on alternative structures, rival authorities, anchorage-points in space and time that were outwith the control of secular governments.

The Church too embraced a diversity of churches. The cult-sites of medieval saints localised religious power firmly at a level below, and often beyond, the reach of the state. In practice cults often consecrated local aristocratic power – there might be a trade-off between bishop or monastery on the one hand, and noble patrons on the other. Yet a cult's constituency could at the same time be 'international'; and the bishop or monastery belonged to an organisation whose head was the pope. Thus the Church embodied alternative power-structures which sometimes legitimised secular power, sometimes collided with it, often spanned and straddled it. But, like secular power itself, the Church's own monarchy was contested from below. Provincial churches and councils challenged papal rulings; local communities did not wait for papal authorisation before venerating new saints; while popular heresy ran alongside and within official ecclesiastical history. Medieval history shows the (often uncomfortable) coexistence of alternative power-sources and power-structures. Recovering such alternatives is an effective antidote to state-centred history or nationalist teleology. Put yourself back in the earlier Middle Ages and you see a world without nations or nationalism, while in the later Middle Ages, you find some nations under construction in a process that was artificial, never biologically given, always contested, sometimes abortive. For most medieval people, identity was a matter of local loyalties; or it was Christendom-wide.

The role of Christianity in the Middle Ages was unique in time. It was also unique in place, and identifies medieval Europe's particularity: because Christian beliefs and practices were shared (and sometimes argued over) throughout Europe, east as well as west, and because Christian churches operated through Europe-wide networks and institutions, the teaching of medieval history cannot be other than resolutely European, transcending (rather than breaking) the national mould. To teach medieval history as national history is an anachronism: to teach one bit of medieval Europe apart from the rest is a contradiction in terms.

Yet the proposals of the History Working Group, perhaps inevitably, given the Secretary of State's specific request 'to increase the emphasis on British history', have a strongly national flavour.[4] European history is assigned no particular place between the ages of seven and eleven, and a relatively minor place between the ages of eleven and fourteen where the Reformation and the Renaissance appear as alternative options along with the French Revolution.[5] Thus no medieval European history at all is prescribed. This omission risks denying pupils an essential part of that very 'understanding of their own cultural roots and shared inheritances' which, according to the Working Group, history should help provide.[6] To exclude them from roots and inheritances that are European just as their future too becomes European seems, in 1990, the very negation of a history that 'must be challenging, relevant and interesting'.[7] With European history as a whole drawing the Working Group's short straw, the possibility of any school's designing a medieval European Study Unit of its own seems remote. The Working Group has avoided Little-Europeanism by leaving Europe little room anywhere at all.

But the alternative to Little-England-ism (which no one wants) is not Little-Europeanism, but Europeanism on the grandest scale. Medieval Europe embraced centre and east as well as west. The Christianity of those regions was far from homogenous: models of organisation, and of relations between church and state, very different from those of England, were offered to medieval Russia along with Orthodox Christianity, by missionaries from Byzantium. Byzantine autocracy was the template of Russian tsardom – but the Byzantine Orthodox Church offered an alternative model too. Monastic cult-sites were focal points of Russian national survival during the Mongol period when no tsar existed. Byzantium also offered face-to-face confrontation between ruler and people as a form of consensus government: parliamentary institutions were not the only way. Byzantine dissent was expressed collectively through anti-acclamations in the great public spaces of the capital city. Mikhael Gorbachev in 1990 in Red Square received a similar message through a similar medium. Eastern Europe at the moment offers other demonstrations of medieval history at its most public and topical. In 1989, a new government in Prague commemorated a heroic self-immolation in Jan Hus Square: the act is resonant for

Czechs because of a fifteenth-century heretic. That same year Serbs commemorated a 600th anniversary - of the battle when the Ottoman Turks overwhelmed the medieval Serbian kingdom. These national histories are parts of European history. Why should British children not know of Hus as well as Becket, Kossovo as well as Hastings? To teach medieval history is to appreciate the dimensions of relevance: political change very often needs to be looked at in the long run.

The Vikings, also recommended for study by the Working Group but only at primary level and in the context of Britain, take us closer to home - but also further away. At the Jorvik Centre in York, the Vikings, wreakers of destruction on a mythic scale, are comfortably incorporated into national history, settling down from rape and pillage to everyday life. The museum's popularity is easy to explain: horror is tamed. The Vikings, domesticated, look like us: family men and free marketeers.[8] There before the visitor's eyes is the local evidence. Jorvik is certainly a good place to start. But the Vikings' activities extended Europe-wide and beyond; and their effects remained ambiguous. Swedes called *Rus*, first documented in the ninth century, traded and settled inland from modern Leningrad, and allied with local Slav princes to found the first Russia.[9] Its wealth came in part from an export known in Western Europe as slaves. In Iceland, the Vikings' 'free state' was an oligarchy which achieved freedom from Norwegian tyrant-kings but kept many of its workforce in slavery: a paradox worth pondering by people of any age or educational stage. But such thoughts can hardly be provoked by studying the Vikings only in Britain. Their history beckons, above all, towards Europe, just as the Scandinavians themselves, in becoming Christian, joined a European political and cultural world as well as an economic one.

The Working Group clearly wanted to open pupils' eyes to the world beyond Europe: a welcome widening of horizons. Thus the Report recommends for eleven-fourteen year-olds the study of Islamic civilisation to the sixteenth century, and of China to the thirteenth century. But those pupils will never have been given the chance to study either western or eastern Christendom at the same period – that is, during the Middle Ages. Surveys of the Orient, denied the possibility of comparison with medieval Europe, float in a vacuum. In the case of Islam, the juxtaposition with Christendom is a historical given. During the first century or so after Muhammed, Arab Muslims were would-be heirs to the Roman Empire, and made the East Roman capital, Constantinople, their prime target. In the eighth century, when Constantinople's survival as the capital of medieval Byzantium was assured, both Islam and Western Christendom created rival imperial centres of their own: thus the empire of Charlemagne based at Aachen was the mirror-image of Harun al Rashid's based at Baghdad. Christian Europe first defined itself as such against Islam.[10] In the case of medieval China, the useful comparison is at the level of historical models: between the vast yet unified Chinese empire, and multicentred Europe; between rulers able to mobilise vast resources on a continuous basis, and rulers whose fairly limited demands were constantly evaded and resisted; between the coherence of Confucian ideology, and the contradictions of Christianity *vis-à-vis* the state. A comparison of the scale-plans of Aachen in 814 (the year of Charlemagne's death), with its barely one square kilometre, contemporary Constantinople's twenty-one, Baghdad's sixty, and Chang'an's seventy-nine, leaves a powerful impression of contrasts to be explained.[11] Unfortunately, neither Charlemagne's empire nor Byzantium gets a look-in anywhere among the Working Group's programmes of study. Pupils reared on a solid English diet with a dash of Oriental spice are missing out on something Continental.

The Working Group stresses the value of history as an intellectual training.[12] Nowhere is this end more attainable than in the medieval field. Distance offers perspective. There are other advantages: nationalism is evidently irrelevant, and racist assumptions can easily be shown to be false. Paradoxically, the fact that documentation is in relatively short supply, especially for the early Middle Ages, is an advantage too – for it means that evidence comes in manageable quantities. Pupils do not have to work (as they inevitably must in the modern field) always with material preselected and packaged by 'experts'. Instead, they can come face-to-face with the difficulties of contemporary, often conflicting, versions as they are. Bias can be appreciated at first hand. Incomplete evidence can be rigorously tested against background knowledge; and the pupil can construct for her/himself 'a coherent account of the past'. A holistic approach is the only possible one: pupils have every incentive to become interdisciplinary. They can use visual materials available in art and architecture and archaeological finds. Local galleries and museums as well as libraries become teaching resources. Literature too offers invaluable historical evidence (as it all too seldom does for pupils studying more modern periods): those whose judgement has been exercised on *Beowulf* or on *The Song of Roland* are practising the historian's craft for themselves.

The reign of Charlemagne is a good example of an earlier medieval subject which serves every single one of the Working Group's 'purposes of school history'. This is a world that pupils at any age can readily recognise: where violence is rarely far below the surface of politics; where image and style count for much; where the dominant personalities are often young people; where brothers compete fiercely for family resources and sons are irked by paternal control. At the same time, this world is remote enough, different enough, to present a huge challenge to the imagination. Charlemagne's people, the Franks, cannot be identified with any modern nation: they were neither 'French' nor 'German', but in some sense the ancestors of both – and of Belgians, Swiss, north Italians and Catalans besides. To imagine the Franks as a people thus requires the shedding of modern 'national' stereotypes. Hunting, engaged in by king and nobility, likewise straddles modern categories: for the Franks, it was a sport and a social ritual, at the same time military exercise, political activity and an essential form of economic provision. The piety of the Franks, and of Charlemagne himself, though manifested in forms that were highly material, defies reduction to material interests: relics were bought dear, and the spoils of war heaped up on the altars of saints. The Franks killed pagan Saxons in the name of Christ – but at least one influential churchman, the Northumbrian Alcuin, protested that paganism in itself was no grounds for killing and that conversion could not be forced.

The study of Charlemagne's reign also has much to offer in terms of intellectual training and the use of historians' distinctive methodology. On major topics – the Franks' wars against the Saxons, for instance, or their contacts with the British Isles, or Charlemagne's coronation as emperor – all or most of the extant evidence can be presented. Two handy collections of the main primary sources in good translations are available – and many of the texts make exhilarating reading.[13] Nets can be cast wide to include art and poetry, tools and weapons, books as objects. Yet there is sufficient documentary material on political and military affairs for pupils to compare official and unofficial accounts, spot deliberate omissions, weigh motive and bias – and in the end, frequently agree to differ on their interpretations.

Further, to study the reign of Charlemagne is to gain both a 'sense of identity' and an 'understanding of cultural roots and shared inheritances', yet, at the same time, to appreciate and respect the 'otherness' of 'other countries and cultures'. The political interests of Charlemagne and of his Frankish followers were served by brutally imposing Christianity (despite Alcuin's protests) on conquered Saxons. Yet Frankish domination also meant the long-term and more peaceful absorption of a common Latin Christian culture throughout an Empire that covered most of western Europe and directly influenced its neighbours not only on the Continent, but also in the British Isles, Scandinavia and Central Europe. Those neighbours participated actively in the Carolingian Empire too, in cultural and religious terms (the Carolingian Renaissance and the extension of Church organisation in Germany are unimaginable without Irish and Anglo-Saxon contributions) and also in economic terms (Scandinavians, Slavs and Spanish Muslims played vital parts in the early medieval economic system – a system which included large numbers of slave-victims but which also had many peasant beneficiaries from participation in markets outwith state control). Charlemagne's reign, in short, was a crucial formative period in a history that British pupils share with their Continental contemporaries. Its omission from a curriculum that has room for 'medieval' Islam, and 'medieval' China, as well as (of course) medieval Britain, seems curiously inappropriate. If pupils are to understand European distinctiveness (with all that implies of destructive and constructive) as they become citizens of the new Europe, do they not need to learn something of the old? The world that Charlemagne and his contemporaries shaped has left its stamp on our own – and it is currently being reshaped before our eyes. In the late twentieth century, could any subject be more 'challenging, relevant and interesting' than the history of the first Europe?

NOTES

1. *National Curriculum History Working Group Final Report, April 1990* (HMSO 1990), pp 36-7, 60-1, 68-9. Cf also p 10, paragraph 3.25, and p 24, paragraphs 5.29-5.31, for the importance of chronological order.

2. *Final Report*, p 1, paragraph 1.7, section vii.

3. S. Reynolds, *Kingdoms and Communities in Western Europe, 900-1300* (1984).

4. *Final Report*, pp 16-17, paragraphs 4.16-4.25.

5. *Final Report*, p 27, List B.

6. *Final Report*, p 1, paragraph 1.7, section iv.

7. *Final Report*, p 2, paragraph 1.9.

8. See P. Addyman and A. Gaynor, 'The Jorvik Viking Centre: an experiment in archaeological site interpretation', *The International Journal of Museum Management and Curatorship* 3 (1984), pp 9-18, and the criticisms of N.A. Chabot, 'The Women of Jorvik', *Archaeological Review from Cambridge*, 7:1 (1988), 67-75.

9. F.D. Logan, *The Vikings in History* (1983).

10. J. Herrin, *The Formation of Christendom*, paperback edn (1989).

11. G. Barraclough ed, *The Times Atlas of World History* (1978) pp 108-9.

12. *Final Report*, p 1, paragraph 1.7, sections vi and vii.

13. H.R. Loyn and J. Percival, *The Reign of Charlemagne* (1975); P.D. King, *Charlemagne. Translated Sources* (1987). Also invaluable is L. Thorpe trans., *Einhard and Notker the Stammerer. Two Lives of Charlemagne* (1969). An excellent textbook for Key Stage 3 pupils would be J. Gillingham, *Charlemagne* (1977), in the Chambers history series, *The Way It Was* (series ed B. Chaplin).

ASA BRIGGS

". . . Most interest with history starts with curiosity about past times. It is seldom, if ever, unrelated, however, to current preoccupations, and when I sat down to answer questions on medieval constitutional history in the week that the Germans invaded Holland and Belgium I did not feel that the examination was well-timed. "

ENGLAND IS A country where interest in history is widespread. There are almost as many newspaper reviews of history books as there are of novels. The mass media present large numbers of history programmes. Historic houses open their doors to thousands of visitors. Ironbridge beckons crowds to explore the origins of the industrial revolution. Schoolchildren produce maps, drawings and even poems for exhibitions relating to their locality. Local history societies thrive, as do family history groups. Every club, every voluntary organisation, celebrates its anniversaries, jubilees and centenaries, often by producing a short history. Towns and cities make the most of their histories in showplaces and festivals. Ancient battles are simulated. The number of business histories multiplies rapidly. History workshops fascinate dedicated members of the labour movement.

It could be – and has been – argued that such preoccupations with the past divert the country from its urgent need to prepare for the future. Yet England is not burdened with the weight of its past as Ireland often seems to be, doubtless in the latter case largely because of what England and Scotland have done to it. Nor are current English preoccupations with the past related to an articulated and assertive nationalism. That there is a latent nationalism that can be roused behind the white cliffs of Dover is beyond doubt, but there is relatively little invention of history to generate feeling. A few dates like 1066 or 55 BC stretch back far in time, but there is a difference between English attitudes to the Battle of Trafalgar and Irish attitudes to the Battle of the Boyne or Scottish attitudes to the Battle of Bannockburn.

In the first and last resort, geography seems to count for more in English national consciousness than history; and the nationalism, although it can be fuelled within the context of the European Community, is largely taken for granted. Public opinion polls classify attitudes that have been determined by influences other than school examination papers in history. In dealing with weighty matters of public policy there is no guarantee that historical experience will be taken into the reckoning. At best it is thought – and said – that 'history teaches lessons'.

Europe is not the only influence on national attitudes. With large-scale immigration during the late twentieth century it is possible to argue that for this reason alone less can and will be taken for granted in the future than at present or in the past. 'The heritage' as handed down from previous generations is now, after all, only one of several heritages. Roots are diverse. Yet there is relatively little effort to achieve mutual knowledge or understanding through knowledge. The implications of living in a multi-cultural society interest only a minority.

The study of history both at school and at university must be considered within this broad national cultural context which reveals many contradictions. So, too, must the debate about the national curriculum in schools, a debate that has involved groups as well as individuals. It is a debate that has followed rather than preceded changes in history curricula in universities, although there are continuing changes in universities themselves. As long ago as 1968 a Fellow of an Oxford college, Brian Harrison, in an important article in *History* described how during the previous decade 'a revolution' had occurred in 'the structure and scope of university history courses'. It has taken time for Oxford itself to catch up.

There have also been big changes in adult education as public interests have changed in recent years – with more emphasis on women's history, on the history of the family and on local and regional history. There has also been an increasing fascination with sources and a greater effort to secure access to information of all kinds, for example through oral history. Everything has become grist to the historian's mill. In the past, as in the early years of R.H. Tawney, tendencies in adult education had influenced tendencies within universities just as much as tendencies in universities had influenced tendencies within adult education. Recently the gap has narrowed. So, if less so, has the gap between 'amateurs' and 'professionals'.

Given this cultural content, the likely future role of history, like its past role, is bound to be a subject for study by cultural historians, fortunately a growing group within the profession. 'Englishness' is now a research topic. It is ironic, therefore, that one of the major university campaigning groups, rightly concerned about the future of history as a university discipline, is called the 'History at

Universities *Defence* Group'. Defence has never seemed to me to be the right word. Nor, indeed, has the word 'universities'. Some of the most interesting and stimulating work on history at the level of higher education is being carried out in polytechnics. Moreover, not all of that work has a local orientation: much of it is comparative and outward-looking. It also draws on a variety of disciplines, as I believe history should.

I am, of course, deeply disturbed by the statistics that the History at Universities Defence Group has collected about the 57 history departments in universities. These show first that, as a result of contraction, 46 of them have no established staff under the age of 30 and, second, that there are many strategic areas of historical scholarship that are not covered at all in some of them. If history does not flourish in universities, there will be serious shortages of people to teach it there and elsewhere. Even more seriously, there will be a shortage of graduates who can bring to their varied professions a knowledge of history, the benefits of which should need no canvassing. The fact that they do need canvassing rightly concerns the History at Universities Defence Group also.

The uses of history as a University subject for the large number of graduates who do not become professional historians are obvious. They can be applied, too, in many different professions. Some of the uses relate to the content of history, some to what have come to be called the 'skills' of the historian – analysing the range and quality of sources of information, including oral and visual information and statistics; assessing bias and reliability; sifting and weighing evidence; weighting a large number of variables; making valid deductions and interpretations from the evidence and avoiding wishful thinking; comparing situations; examining change both at home and 'abroad'; and presenting findings in a cogent and effective manner.

Such skills are marketable. The content, too, is in many, if not in all cases, relevant to working and living in the twentieth century. Business studies usually include a case history component. Diplomacy benefits from a knowledge of historical facts and forces. The media are called upon to relate the news of the present and the options for the future to information about the past. For these reasons deficiencies in business, diplomacy and journalism can often be traced back to a lack of historical knowledge as well as to a lack of historical perspective.

The question of what kind of history is being studied in higher education, particularly in universities, has far wider bearings, therefore, than the production of future history teachers, essential though that production is; and when Harrison surveyed what history was being studied in 1968 – and how – he was right, I believe, to use the word 'revolution'. The kind of history that was already being taught there in 1968 often highly effectively – was a far broader kind of history than had been taught before the 1960s, the most controversial decade of this century.

I myself was brought up as an undergraduate on Cambridge constitutional history, a large part of it medieval, and what I learnt of the twentieth century was confined to 'the theory of the modern state'. I did not write a single essay on Victorian England. As a modern historian I have not suffered greatly in consequence, partly because in Sir Ernest Barker I had a superb tutor, who could deal with any topic in history, and partly because through a special subject on Utilitarianism and Tory Democracy I secured an entry into territories of political, economic, social and cultural history that I have explored ever since. The course, however, was not well suited to the needs and interests of students who were not aspiring to become professional historians, 'the weaker vessels' as one Cambridge lecturer referred to them condescendingly; and even as an undergraduate living in difficult times when historical events were moving fast, I found myself drawn into arguments for curricular reform. We all recognised, of course, that much depended on the qualities of our tutors. In those universities where lectures were the staple means of instruction – and there were many of these – students could be less fortunate.

What interested me most in history then was exploring, and I believed then, as I do now, that most interest in history starts with curiosity about past times. It is seldom, if ever, unrelated, however, to current preoccupations, and when I sat down to answer questions on medieval constitutional history in the week that the Germans invaded Holland and Belgium I did not feel that the examination was well-timed. In the light of events in central and eastern Europe and in the Soviet Union since 1989 – not to speak of Canada – constitutional history would now be better timed and placed.

There are some students of history whose approach is different from mine and who start not with curiosity about the past but with concern about how to act in the present. When they go on to talk of the 'lessons of history', as do Members of Parliament and even Prime Ministers, they are on shaky ground, as Professor Michael Howard pointed out in his inaugural lecture as Regius Professor of Modern History at Oxford in 1981. He was right then to insist that the first lesson that historians teach – and it is they, not 'History' who are the teachers – is an austere one 'not to generalise from false premises based on inadequate evidence'.

Another thing that I learnt is that history is a matter not of agreement but of debate. Just as men and women often disagree in the present, so they often disagreed in the past, and historians will continue to disagree when they examine their ancestors' disagreements. We cannot reach finality, as, for example, Sir Lewis Namier seemed at times to believe that we could. There are some facts which all historians will accept, but even these facts are themselves subject to revision in the light of new evidence. Those people, whether in authority or in rebellion against it, who want history to mean the same for everyone, are bound to be frustrated and disappointed by what historians say and do. I start from the premise that history is now a far livelier subject than it was when I was an undergraduate.

It was the immense variety of history syllabuses as much as the indifferent quality of teaching in some schools which encouraged the idea of a national curriculum in history within a core curriculum and which led to the publication of the Report of the National History Working Group which now figures as the entry point into current debate.

The Report of the History Working Group, which is limited to courses from primary school through to sixteen and how best to teach them, is full, perhaps over full, or rather over long, and well balanced, and it lays just the right emphasis, I believe, on the place of 'knowledge in the sense of content' in all school history courses. History is a knowledge-based subject, and it is impossible to dispense with 'facts'. Moreover, a knowledge of the order in which things happened or were thought to have happened is central to the whole study of the subject. History is about time and the best historians are good time travellers. As the Report says 'Chronology . . . provides a mental framework or map which gives significance and coherence to the study of history. A school history course should respect chronology and be broadly chronological in structure.'

Too many existing school history 'courses' are fragmented, while in some schools history is merely one element in a mixed 'humanities' course which even the best teachers, including those who have devised it, find difficult to hold together. It is impossible to develop through such a course any understanding of the significance of detail, the kind of detail of ideas, events and processes that it is essential to appreciate. History, therefore, should be treated as a distinctive discipline within a cluster of related disciplines rather than subsumed in an unwieldy package. There has to be a 'coherence of structure'.

I have never approved of rigid 'departmentalism' either in schools or in higher education, but before effective 'interdisciplinarity' can be achieved – and it is necessary if we are to understand 'problems' and how to cope with them – there has to be an encounter with particular disciplines. I agree with the History Working Group that 'history is a subject of immense breadth which can both inform, and draw upon other areas of the curriculum, including languages. I believe also that the influence (and it should be a reciprocal one) relates as much to literature, art and music as to the social sciences. A whole chapter of the Report is rightly devoted to 'the relationship of history to the rest of the curriculum'.

I am rather less sure, however, about the conclusions of the Report in relation to the primary school curriculum, and even in relation to the secondary curriculum I would wish to emphasise the importance of Chapter 10 on 'bringing history to life'. The best kind of primary school education in history already sets a high standard. It is designed, like the best kind of university education in history, to persuade learners to learn for themselves through exploration. I trace a great arc between primary school education in history and university, polytechnic and adult education in history. The need at both ends is to be enthused.

The structured history syllabus associated with the first three years of work in secondary schools, when, according to the Report, history achieves its 'most secure position in the curriculum', should be well structured just because these years follow up an earlier phase of exploration and in a minority of cases provides a foundation for a second exploratory phase in higher education. By contrast, history for adults can draw heavily not only on the desire to explore but on actual experience. Only then can history become a really 'mature' subject.

I note that there is only a brief reference to the penultimate phase of education before that last phase is reached – also a phase outside the Working Party's remit – 'history for pupils aged sixteen to nineteen'. 'For the first time,' the Report remarks, 'those who plan curricula for the sixteen to nineteen age group will have a predictable base on which to rest their policies in terms of the historical information, understanding and skills that pupils will have been taught up to the age of sixteen.' This deals correctly with the lead-in to the phase. As for what happens within it, in my view, the approach to history in the crucial years between sixteen to nineteen should not be determined solely by the academic demands of the universities. Given that a substantial section of the small minority group then at school or college will not go on to university, attention should be paid to the needs of the whole group and not just to a part of it.

During these years there is scope both for relating history to other disciplines and for a co-ordinated approach to the issues of contemporary British society and of the contemporary world seen in perspective. Yet there should be an attractive element of competition in the range of courses provided: they should appeal to many tastes. The interests and needs of different pupils, then in the course of articulation, will necessarily diverge. It will be particularly necessary, during these years to ensure that history continues to be 'brought to life'. At present, far too many teachers still believe, or imply that they believe, that the best way to deal with the subject is to rely on notes and guidance about reading, the latter too heavily associated with textbooks. Inspectors' reports suggest that there is urgent need for reform. The view that historical examining at this stage merely means ticking off points and giving marks for them provides them with far too easy a justification. Attentive judgements should be encouraged, not inhibited.

'Delivering history by different strategies' is the title, topical in its language, of one of the sub-sections of the key chapter on 'implementation' which rightly begins with 'resources'. There is no point in producing a blueprint for education in history at any level of school, college, university or polytechnic education unless attention is paid to resources. Will there be enough teachers? Will they have the right qualifications? Will they be motivated to make the implementation of a particular blueprint feasible? (Without them it can never be.) Will they have the right library, video and other resources at their disposal? In education means are often as important as ends, although there will inevitably be disagreement as to just what means are necessary.

The study of history itself should enable such questions to be seen in perspective and answered intelligently, if the claims made for history as a distinctive academic subject are justified. In my view nothing will be gained by concentration on a limited debate on modes of assessment or on narrow attempts 'to defend [again a dangerous word] the integrity of history as a shool subject'. Its claims to be an essential part of the core curriculum are too wide-ranging for that. And what happens at school is important primarily in relation to what comes afterwards. It was Sir Keith Joseph himself who said in 1984 that 'history properly taught justifies its place in the curriculum by what it does to prepare all pupils for the responsibilities of citizenship as well as the demands of employment and the opportunities of leisure'.

RAPHAEL SAMUEL

" 'Knowledge with understanding' may be more confusing than rote-learning, but history is an argument about the past as well as the record of it: from the point of view of the learning process, giving the right answers seems less important than asking interesting questions, hypothesising connections, and making a continuous narrative out of fragments. "

ONE OF THE distinctive features of the current debate about history – novel, strange and perhaps for practitioners of the subject, a little frightening – is that it is not about what happened in the past, and the relative importance of this or that event, as the Norman Conquest, say, or the Coronation Oath of Henry IV. Nor, as in such remembered controversies as those surrounding the rise of the gentry, or the origins of the Second World War, is it about how the past should be interpreted. It is not even, except intermittently, about the rival claims of 'history from above' and 'history from below', the great point of divide when the 'new wave' histories of the 1960s challenged the ruling orthodoxy . It is rather about who we are, where we come from and how we relate to a world changing so dramatically before our eyes.

If there is a single issue which has made history into a front-line subject and propelled it into the arena of public debate, it is the question of what it means, in the present day, to be British. In recent decades, the national question has emerged, or re-emerged, as a storm-centre of British politics, most obviously in relation to New Commonwealth immigration and settlement, and Britain's membership of the EEC.

The civil war in Ulster, now in its twenty-third year, the recrudescence of Celtic separatism, and the Assembly movement in Scotland, has put the break-up of Britain on the agenda of practical politics. Conversely the 'heritage' industry and the commodification of the national past, has contrived to make the idea of 'Englishness' aesthetically and visually appealing at the very moment when, with the collapse of industry and the withdrawal from Empire, it appears politically and economically bankrupt. It is not surprising that education has felt these tremors, and the urgency with which the national curriculum has been pursued, and the support it has won from politicians of all stripes, owes something to the fear that, left to itself, the country is falling apart.

For Conservatives, the restoration of history to the core curriculum is a way of calling up a lost sense of something indigenous, restoring a sense of unity, or at any rate continuity, in national life, reaffirming a sense of national onenesss. For many radicals, anyway those who have espoused the cause of anti-racism, or who, under the influence of the 'global village' idea of the 1960s, have adopted a 'world studies' approach to the subject, it is a way of challenging xenophobia and insularity. For liberal educators, like the HMI and the History Working Group, it is a way of promoting 'tolerance and respect for cultural variety'; on the one hand giving pupils 'a sense of identity' and 'an understanding of their own roots', on the other encouraging attitudes of respect for others.

I do not believe these different aims are as incompatible as they seem. In any event, since they represent major currents of teacherly opinion, and competing versions of teaching practice, each has its own legitimacy, and the new core curriculum should be plural enough to give each its head. But these issues need arguing. *Not* to teach British history has been, for a whole generation of teachers, a very inspiration of their work. If British history is now to be the core of the new core curriculum – as I believe it should be – a case has to be made with equal conviction.

The History Working Group, in a valiant attempt to maintain balance and to accommodate the views of globalists and nationalists without surrendering to either, sidestep the issue. Bending to the Minister's will they have increased from 40 to 50 per cent the time-table hours devoted to the teaching of British history. But they are less than enthusiastic about this, arguing that an understanding of British history should be the 'foundation' of pupils' learning, 'since it is the main framework of their immediate experience', but then going on to make the case for European history, and for 'world' history in similar terms. Neither the case for British history nor its peculiar difficulties and excitement, nor the explosive tensions attaching to the idea of nation, both in the present and the past, are argued out, with the result that the syllabus is robbed of what might have been one of its unifying problematics.

On the issue of 'skills' versus 'knowledge', too, the Working Group – declaring that the debate is 'irrelevant' – finds itself facing both ways. On the one hand, resisting ministerial pressure for names and dates and facts, they argue for the primacy of 'understanding', point to the opacity of the term 'knowledge' and steer clear of using it, as though it had been in some sort contaminated. On the other hand, as enthusiasts for the subject, they are insistent on the need for 'historical information' and prescribe a staggering quantity of 'essential' and 'exemplary' 'information' which – to meet the attainment targets in the syllabus – pupils are expected to master.

In spite of well-advertised differences, the consultation exercise has shown a remarkable amount of common ground on the content of a new syllabus, and the competing claims of local, national and global history. Here the Working Group's pluralist approach has been widely endorsed, even by some of its fiercest critics. It has established something like a consensus on a 'Four nations' approach to the national past (still a novelty when the Working Group made its Interim report). It has forced the history of Empire onto the cognitive map (in the Interim report it was omitted). It has shown near unanimity amongst teachers on the inseparability of interpretation, understanding and knowledge – the issue conspicuously dividing the Working Group and the Minister.

But the consultation exercise has raised as many questions as it has resolved. For one thing it has exposed a chasm of misunderstanding between history in the universities and history in the schools. By and large the Working Group report was warmly welcomed in university history departments, and there was a positive eagerness to make some contribution to the success of the new syllabus. In the schools, to judge by the workshops and conferences held throughout the country and by the correspondence columns of *The Times Educational Supplement* and elsewhere, the response has been much more guarded, and the manner in which the national curriculum has been imposed – a top-down reform making little attempt to draw upon examples of best practice – has fuelled suspicion that, far from marking a new deal for history, it represents a further stage in the de-skilling of the teacher's work.

Then there is the vexed question of the status of history as a discipline and as a separate teaching subject. The university history departments, who see their job as training apprentice historians, seem to be at odds with the professionalism – and the idealism – of the Institutes of Education who have the job of training graduate teachers, and who have been one of the nurseries of 'New' history in the schools. Focusing attention on children's needs, and on the 'ages' and 'stages' of the learning process, the Institutes have been suspicious of subject specialisms and have aimed to produce teachers who were in the first place 'educationalists'. But the vocation of historian, whatever the arguments which can be advanced against history as an autonomous field of knowledge, is not one to be given up lightly. It has the advantage of enjoying public respect and in the past did a great deal to shore up the teacher's sense of authority and worth, as someone with a knowledge to impart. It is a title proudly adopted by the thousands of people engaged in such 'do-it-yourself' projects as those in local history and family history. And once upon a time it had the merit of uniting school teachers and university teachers in a sense of common cause.

The public debate, and the consultation process, have shown the impossibility of returning to the old history, or of attempting to impose an Authorized Version of the national past, even if the government were minded to do so. For one thing many of the old landmarks – such as Parliament and the two-Party system – have lost their lustre, and could hardly appear as pinnacles of national achievement – the place they occupied in the constitutional history of yesteryear. Then, the idea of an Anglo-centric history seems to be regarded with universal derision, and would be difficult to reinstate on the eve of Britain's entry into the European Monetary Union. Famous names and dates would also be difficult to restore to their former place of honour. As the Working Group report showed, and as the consultation process confirmed, the place of local history and of project work – and within it the use of oral history – is now so firmly established in school practice, from the youngest age-groups onwards, that it is no longer even controversial.

The debate has also, in my view, shown some of the limitations of 'history from below', and of the 'patch' approach with which, in recent times, it has been associated. Deprived of its adversary – 'Drum-and-Trumpet history', or history as the biography of great men – it loses its subversive potential. Enlarging the subject matter of history in some spheres it can narrow it in others. By privileging the local and the familial, it has nothing to say about international relations and indeed very little about the nation as a whole, let alone – an integral part of 'our Island Story' which left-wing historians in recent years have sadly neglected – the British Empire. By focusing on the everyday and the ordinary it has no imaginative space for those sensational occurrences, extreme situations and memorable characters which have always fascinated historians and have quite largely accounted for the subject's popular (and class-room) appeal. Then, by valorising history in depth at the expense of history in breadth it has removed what used to be one of the great strengths of Marxist and radical historiography in this country, that of the broad interpretative narrative or framework. Finally by confining its major effort to the nineteenth and twentieth centuries it is poorly equipped to address the national question as it presents itself in earlier times.

It would be a great pity if, in search of performance indicators or attainment tests, such as the new 'core' curriculum prescribes –

or for that matter in pursuit of the 'New' history's 'skill' levels and 'concepts' – the syllabus were to lock children up in a problematic of pedagogy's own making. One of the great strengths of school history, by comparison with the universities, is that it has normally been much more sensitive to changes, and tensions, in the society at large. It has been less afraid of asking the big questions and also of recognising that, whatever our beliefs in ethical neutrality, history is an arena for moral argument. It has also often been more hospitable to changes in historical knowledge. Through the medium of such inspired texts as the Quennell's *History of Everyday Things* (1919) social history won a place in the junior school some fifty years before it gained recognition in the universities. The schools have been more ready than the universities to make use of the County Record Offices and to treat the criticism of original documents as a normal part of class-room practice. And they have been much more receptive to the use of both oral testimony and visual artefacts as historical sources. It is also from the schools that the pressure has come to address the history of Empire. Mary Seacole's autobiography, long forgotten, now reprinted – the life of a British Caribbean who travelled in three continents and set up a nursing station during the Crimean war – is a sight more interesting than the *Sir Robert Peel from his private papers,* or even Carlyle's *Chartism*, as an introduction to early Victorian Britain. If it is now quite widely known it is because of the efforts of the Tulse Hill schoolmasters who pioneered study of the black presence in Britain and those obscure presses who have seconded their efforts.

If there is to be a dialogue between schools and universities it needs to be a two-way affair, one in which universities take inspiration and example from schools, as well as upholding, according to their own lights, 'traditional' standards. The universities have as much to learn as to give. Conversely, it would be self-defeating if, in deference to child-centred learning or do-it-yourself projects, school history were to cut itself off from higher research. Whether as a knowledge-based subject or an evidence-derived discipline, history depends on – or at any rate is finally limited by – the findings of empirical work, and in the schools as elswhere it needs people who take some pride in the vocation of historian. It does no service either to the teachers or the taught to suggest that they are on a par with each other, or that teachers are no more than 'enablers'. The idea of knowledge, like that of history, is an honourable and ancient one: there is no reason why it should suddenly become shamefaced.

We live in an expanding historical culture, in which vast new fields of enquiry compete for attention, and whole new classes of evidence are being brought into play. It would be absurd if school history were to turn its back on this, or to ignore the growing points of public interest in and engagement with, the past. Nor, for the sake of producing testable facts, should it return to a naïve empiricism when the status of knowledge is being questioned in every field of thought. To do so would be to deprive the subject of one of its principal contemporary excitements, that of engaging with the role of memory and myth in the making of historical narrative. 'Knowledge with understanding' may be more confusing than rote-learning, but history is an argument about the past as well as the record of it; from the point of view of the learning process, giving the right answers seems less important than asking interesting questions, hypothesising connections, and making a continuous narrative out of fragments.

Syllabuses exist to be subverted. The vitality of history as a teaching subject whether in the universities or in the schools, has always depended on an ability to transcend them, or to develop new initiatives on the side. A syllabus can usefully protect pupils from being at the mercy of the teacher's whim, or from being delivered up to the fashions of the day. But a syllabus has no principle of growth and in a subject which is forever changing its boundaries, it is inevitably – like the rival topics currently on offer – out of date. School history cannot be insulated from changes in attitudes to the past, nor can its content be settled by ministerial memos. If children in primary schools are even today, given the 'Three-Field system' to draw, as a way of initiating them into medieval England, it is because of the enormous imaginative success of the Orwin's *Open Fields* – the work of two agrarian radicals, combining field work and archive research to document a disappearing world.

No committee, even one as ecumenically-minded as the DES History Working Group, has either the resources or the capacity to legislate the shape of history for the decade to come. In the end it will depend on the ways in which history is exhibited and staged; the manner in which it surfaces in issues of public controversy; the urgency or otherwise of the books we write and the projects we take part in.

F. M. L. THOMPSON

" The Great War, as it used to be called, clearly did break out in 1914, but no amount of listing, tracing, and describing of the multiple conflicts, fears and ambitions which contributed to that event can ever result in an irrefutably correct explanation of the catastrophe . . . "

THE MATERIALISTS, the technocrats, and the single-issue men are on the march. In the climate of crude individualism, reverence for market forces, and unabashed self-indulgence which has flourished in the last ten years, the hardfaced businessmen who have done well under Mrs Thatcher have come out of the woodwork and denounced the education system as being responsible for all Britain's economic troubles (as well, presumably, as being responsible for their own good fortune, although they seldom say this). The most recent outburst comes from the Director-General of the Institute of Directors, Peter Morgan, who is reported as saying that: 'The pernicious influence of the academic mould is not an accidental side effect; it is the direct outcome of education policies continuously pursued by the academic establishment and the pontificating classes which the system produced. On the one hand an élite has been produced which is alienated from business, commerce and industry; on the other hand, at the opposite end of the scale, nearly half of the school leaving population has just been plain alienated' (*The Independent*, 29 June 1990). What he wants is an education system centred on vocational training, on the grounds that the purpose of education is to help us earn a living, not to humanise our inner nature; as though the two were incompatible. While this broad frontal attack sweeps on, nourished by appeals to parental power coupled with unbelievably shortsighted official parsimony towards the school system we have, the single-issue men grind away on the astonishingly narrow front of the meaning of the concept of knowledge and the way in which the quantity of it possessed by schoolchildren ought to be tested, seemingly oblivious of the consequences which their campaign may have for what is to be taught in our schools. In times like these it is extremely important that there should be a properly informed and responsible debate about school subjects, and that the future of the educational system should not be left by default to the pontifications either of businessmen or of single-track zealots.

What has all this to do with history, particularly with the scheme for history in the schools proposed in the Final Report of the History Working Group? A lot. The notion that education should be practical, utilitarian, vocational, and sold in packages promising increased earning-power, has a hard-headed, no-nonsense, ring to it, dismissive of airy-fairy subjects which have no obvious direct applications in 'real life' or in 'the outside world'. These are favourite phrases with those who want us to believe that there is one lot of subjects that are of 'purely academic interest' whose adherents live in an ivory tower remote from the hurly-burly of the real world, and another lot that are concerned with the serious business of wealth creation. On inspection this turns out to be empty rhetoric. On practical grounds it is impossible to give vocational training to seven-year-olds, unless their vocations are pre-ordained by birth and social circumstances in the way that the occupations of Victorian children at straw-plaiting schools were pre-ordained. It is an equal nonsense to try to provide job-specific education and training for sixteen-year-olds, except in a command economy capable of accurate prediction of manpower requirements, and such a paragon has never existed. Of far greater importance, the confusion of vocational training with education is misleading and potentially disastrous. There is no one single tool kit or set of spanners appropriate for the operation of all the different bits of machinery of the economy; each job or range of jobs has its own set, and it is the business of vocational training to learn about a particular tool kit and how to use it, at the appropriate stage in growing up. The preparation for learning this is a broad and general education which, if it has done its job, will have helped produce adaptable, flexible, imaginative, and well-stocked minds. The rights of the individual and the needs of society converge in requiring that this general education should help to discover, bring out, and develop the potential abilities of every schoolchild.

History is an essential, central element in this broad and general education. Of course it is not the only one, and the necessity of learning the fundamentals of literacy, numeracy, and basic scientific method is undisputed; and the 'fundamentals' in question are infinitely more sophisticated than the three R's which the Victorians thought would suffice for the needs of the masses. These subjects, however, deal in precision, certainty, predictability, and objectivity, in the right way of doing things and the wrong way, in the right answers and the wrong answers. It is indeed healthy to learn that two and two make four, and it can be embarrassing not to spell embarrassing correctly. Particularly in the mathematical and natural sciences the notions of probability, uncertainty, and accident are scarcely encountered until sixth-form or university level work. History is alone in having both a subject matter which introduces issues of credibility, plausibility, and probability as well as degrees of certainty, and a method of disciplined study which deals in arguments and interpretations not in cut and dried answers and proofs. The Norman Conquest did happen in 1066, but we cannot say with complete certainty why William decided to invade or why he won; opinions can be formed on the basis of the surviving evidence, which itself needs to be sifted and tested for reliability, and on the whole the better informed the opinion the more convincing it will be. Charles I certainly had his head cut off in 1649, but that is an event capable of being understood and explained at very many different levels and no amount of evidence can provide a single 'correct' answer to the question why it happened. The Great War, as it used to be called, clearly did break out in 1914, but no amount of listing, tracing, and describing of the multiple conflicts, fears, and ambitions which contributed to that event can ever result in an irrefutably correct explanation of the catastrophe, although it can sort out explanations into those which are perverse, inadequate, or distorted, and those which seem probable and consistent with all the known evidence.

There is no need for further illustrations. History is about what people have done in the past. In the past, as in the present, people did things for very complicated reasons in which the apparently illogical and irrational was mixed with the rational, and in which chance and accident, sometimes from natural causes like the weather and sometimes through the intervention of other individuals, played a part. Faced with studying and trying to understand the complexities and vagaries of people in the past, their blunders, muddles, mistakes, and disasters, as well as their triumphs and achievements, any student of history is bound to become aware both of the curious twists and turns of human behaviour and its consequences, and of the challenge of attempting to make sense of it all. Respect for the evidence, and a critical, questioning attitude towards its meaning, go hand in hand, and this goes for all ages and all levels of study: there is not, in the study of history, any division between a junior period during which rules and answers are simply taught and learnt, and an adult period in which independent thought and criticism are permitted and encouraged. At the end of the process of studying history, in the system of formal education, eminently employable people emerge with highly marketable skills in habits of analysis, discrimination between fact and opinion, testing of received wisdom, and awareness of the importance of communicating, skills which are sought after in the City, in commerce and industry, in government, in the media, as well as in the education system itself. There is no need for Peter Morgan to be worried that this kind of education is wasteful, is lacking in relevance to the real world; on the contrary, it helps to provide precisely the kind of talents which keep the real world going.

That may come at the end of an education running through to degree level. But at earlier ages and stages in the study of history the qualities of being able to find out for oneself and think for oneself are stimulated and developed through looking at and learning about bodies of information which have to be sifted and sorted for reliability, accuracy, relevance, generality, typicality, bias, partiality, and many other features. Above all, this information is acquired in satisfaction of a curiosity about how things got to be how they are which is so widespread as to be practically universal. The curiosity of children may be fired by things which they see or feel around them, still existing in the present, like buildings, factories, road systems, or field patterns, or institutions like the schools they are in, churches, local councils, sports clubs, Parliament, and Government; but it may equally be fired by things long defunct, seen in museums or reflected in legends and myths, heard of in storybooks or glimpsed in TV costume dramas. History is an extremely good curiosity-driven subject, a splendid way of harnessing the enthusiasm, excitement, and sheer fun of finding out to the cultivation of habits of orderly, disciplined, and structured enquiry. It is natural that curiosity about things which have a past should be directed at first to the country in which one lives, and should be led on to questions about peoples and influences coming from outside, and so to curiosity about other peoples and other regions for their own sake. In British schools it is natural and essential that British history should occupy a large place in a history syllabus: this may incidentally be important because it teaches people who and what they are in terms of the society and country in which they live, and because it preserves and transmits some concept of national identity, but it is primarily important because the immediacy and tangibility of the past is most obviously experienced in that way, and attention is most likely to be aroused and retained. Inquisitiveness about other peoples and other countries is perhaps more of an acquired taste, which needs a certain amount of fostering by teachers. Once discovered, whether in the flesh, in lessons, or in books, foreign places may easily become more interesting and exciting than home, and the danger becomes that the mysteries of China or Peru, not to mention the charms of France, may crowd out due attention to a coherent pattern of study and turn history into a magpie's nest or lucky dip. The first essential, however, is to establish that doing proper history is enjoyable, using facts and dates and places as building bricks for understanding what has happened in the past, how and why and with what effects on what came after. When that is accomplished the reining in of possibly unbridled and undirected curiosity to the confines of what is reasonable, practicable, and coherent as a feasible programme of study becomes a matter of compromises, adjustments, and selections, which are as much to do with the availability of school time and resources as they are to do with intellectual priorities.

In all this the Final Report of the History Working Group has an excellent grip on the heart of the matter, and its proposals point the way to an exciting and flourishing future for history in the schools, provided more resources are put into its teaching – in teachers, in refresher courses, in books, in field trips. There are, and will be, wrangles over its selection of subjects and topics, objections to its omission of this and objections to its inclusion of that. It may well be that a different group of legislators would have come up with a different, but equally imperfect, set of subjects to be studied: a bit more British history, or a bit more European history, or a bit more extra-European history, or a bit more twentieth-century history, or a bit more medieval history, or less stress on social history, or less prominence for political history, or less space for long-period themes. The possibilities for counter-suggestions are almost endless, and the possibility of achieving a programme to suit all tastes and all opinions non-existent. The important points about the range and content of the Study Units in the Report are that they strike an acceptable and workable balance between core subjects and optional subjects; that they provide for a reasonable balance between British and non-British history, and between different chronological periods; that they avoid any devaluation of the intellectual capital of existing schoolteachers by providing ample openings for school-devised Units; and above all, that they constitute a scheme which can be put into action, to the great benefit of many schools and many children for whom anything recognisable as history scarcely exists at present, a scheme which will not be cast in concrete for all time but which can be, and must be, reviewed and adjusted in the light of experience.

While it is unlikely that anyone will go out of their way to claim that the proposals are perfect in terms of content, it cannot be said too strongly or too loudly that the Working Group has got the purposes of school history absolutely right. The wording of the Report is maybe a trifle solemn on the matter, and it would have been good to have been reminded that the training of the mind in disciplined enquiry, the acquisition of a sense of identity, the understanding of other countries, and so forth are qualities and skills which it is positively enjoyable to develop through the study of history. But documents designed to convince governments which like to pretend they are sternly Victorianised can hardly argue that the serious business of education is also fun, even intellectualised fun. The Report is excellent, too, on the essence of history, and it is worth quoting its emphasis on 'an education which instils a respect for evidence', and its clear statement 'that there is no final answer to any historical question: and that there are no monopolies of the truth'.

It is this, however, which has led the Report into its greatest troubles and subjected it to a battering which must have left its authors somewhat bemused. This has arisen because some amiable and well-meaning people have become intoxicated by the ambiguities of their own rhetoric about history as a knowledge-based subject and the necessity of testing historical knowledge when assessing pupils' attainments in the subject. The Report is in fact entirely clear that history is knowledge-based, that being almost a truism. It is equally clear that while 'knowledge' is a good old-fashioned, robust word, it commonly is used to mean different things: 'information', 'understanding', and 'content'. It is true that among a relatively small group of people who understand each other's ways, such as the community of university historians, the single word 'knowledge' can be, and is, ordinarily used in different meanings in different contexts and is perfectly well understood by all concerned without any ambiguity. Thus, university lecturers and examiners may say that A has a better knowledge of the 1931 crisis and slump than B, and give A higher marks than B; meaning not that A knows 10 or a 100 more facts about the crisis and slump than B, but that A understands its origins, course, and consequences better than B, possibly in the process of showing better understanding also deploying more facts than B and certainly showing the inter-relationship of a collection of facts more perspicaciously. That is fine within a network whose sense of shared assumptions and common standards have been built up over many years. When it comes to legislating for thousands of teachers and thousands of schools and many age groups, however, it is advisable to avoid using words which may be misinterpreted, and to stick to terms which have been precisely defined even at the risk of appearing pedantic. That is all that the Final Report has done. History, it says, is not about collecting a basketful of facts, but about understanding the meaning and significance of facts. Testing history is not about scoring points for memorising information, but about assessing how far and in what ways information has been understood and digested. Since that is what good teachers, whether in schools or in universities, have always done when assessing the 'knowledge' or 'command' of a subject, it is difficult to see why anyone should object to seeing the process and criteria of assessment spelled out in the terminology of 'understanding', 'evaluating', and 'organising' historical information, which is the vocabulary adopted in the Report.

The debate will no doubt continue to smoulder on, for emotions and sentiments are involved which will not easily cool down. But the Working Group surely deserves congratulations on their labours, which promise to put history firmly into the schools, not brickbats.

P.J. MARSHALL

"It would . . . be a sign of the maturity of British society if young British people could learn to look at the imperial past as an historical problem to be judged like other problems, rather than one which evokes automatic and unthinking affirmations of loyalty or rejection."

IT IS NO DOUBT an occupational hazard for academics to be complacent about the current state of the particular branch of the discipline that they happen to study. Nevertheless, while having to declare a personal interest in its current well-being, it still seems to be a fair conclusion that the study of the British imperial past attracts scholarship of some distinction and that a considerable number of students in higher education evidently enjoy learning about it. It is taught successfully both in universities and in polytechnics. For instance, at the Polytechnic of North London, courses on the Victorian Empire and the British Empire and Commonwealth appear to be among the most popular on offer in the School of History.

Even the complacent insider must, however, recognise limitations. Great surveys of the imperial past, starting from some point as far back as the sixteenth century, are now distinctly out of fashion. Recent studies have become more narrowly focused, both in time and in area. Relatively few scholars now profess competence in more than one broad geographical region and the historiography of the British empire tends as a result to be something of a mosaic of separate area studies. The subject has fragmented and its coverage tends to be uneven. Some periods and some parts of the empire are now much more closely studied than others. A vast amount has, for instance, recently been written on the end of empire after the Second World War and on the history of British India. By contrast, little has recently appeared in Britain on Australia, New Zealand or Canada.

Even if it is fragmented, the subject still keeps an essential coherence through study of the common British denominator and thus of the interaction between the history of Britain and the histories of those peoples brought within the orbit of British expansion.[1] If the vitality of any academic discipline can in part be deduced from its capacity to generate controversy, study of the imperial past is in good health. For instance, publication in 1986 of an ambitious book by Lance Davis and R. Huttenback, called *Mammon and the Pursuit of Empire*, has set off wide-ranging debates about the costs and benefits of empire to Britain in the late nineteenth and early twentieth centuries.[2]

Although such debates may be vigorous, they do not seem to involve very fundamental ideological disagreements. The point of view of the academic imperial historian seems now to vary from what might be regarded as a liberal–conservative position to positions further left. As Shula Marks has noted, the recent historiography of empire seems not to be either 'celebratory' or 'apologetic' about the past.[3] This does not mean that claims to detect a hidden imperial agenda are not sometimes made, as for example by Indian critics of western writing on Indian living standards under colonial rule or on the origins of nationalism. Professed and overt imperialists have, however, dropped out of academic life, as they seem to have dropped out of national politics. Contrary to popular belief, the substance of serious imperialism in its heyday was always much more concerned with the possibilities of integrating 'white' communities into a larger British military and economic bloc than with the urge to rule yet more peoples. Integration into NATO and the EEC has finally dispelled any lingering hopes of a free-standing Great Britain, sustained by the resources of an empire/Commonwealth. The contemporary Commonwealth evidently retains the goodwill of most academics as it does of most politicians. The political right, however, where vestigial imperialism might perhaps have been expected to linger, appears often to regard the Commonwealth with some irritation as a potential threat to the exercise of full national sovereignty, a claimant to economic preferences in a free-market world and a source of unwelcome immigrants. In 1972, for instance, Mr Enoch Powell seemed to be turning his back on his own imperial past when he dismissed citizens of Commonwealth countries as people who had 'no more connection or affinity with the United Kingdom than with China or Peru'.[4]

That a subject can hold its own in higher education is not of course a necessary reason why it should be taught in schools. In the case of the history of the British empire there may indeed be serious difficulties in presenting it as a school subject. The complexities of some of the issues are likely to be extremely daunting for younger pupils and issues which no longer disturb academics, who appear to accept a rough consensus that the impact of British imperialism is either to be deplored or not to be overtly celebrated, may still strike deep resonances in

certain sections of British society and arouse corrosive antagonisms.

Nevertheless, in his guidance to the chairman of the Working
Group set up in 1989 to advise on a national curriculum for history,
the then Secretary of State for Education and Science, Kenneth
Baker, urged the Group to produce programmes of study that 'take
account' of Britain's 'changing role as a European, Commonwealth
and world power'. In its Final Report the Group recommend that
the history of the British empire be studied in several different forms.
'Exploration. Drake. Raleigh' are included as 'essential information'
for the programmes on 'Life in Tudor and Stuart England' for children from seven to eleven. World-wide commercial and imperial
expansion appears in two of the 'core' units of British history at key
stage three (children from eleven to fourteen). At the same key stage
the British presence overseas features largely in the optional units on
India, the American Revolution and 'Black peoples of the Americas',
while there is also a separate unit on the 'British empire at its zenith'.
In key stage four (for pupils from fourteen to sixteen) imperial and
Commonwealth issues are elements in the British core unit for the
twentieth century. The transition from colonialism to independence
are major themes in the optional units on modern South Asia and
Africa. In short, if these proposals are adopted, pupils can hardly
avoid encountering references to the imperial past in the compulsory
curriculum and there will be opportunities for them to learn about
it in some detail if they choose certain options.

The case for at least some treatment of the history of empire in
any national history curriculum rests on a number of considerations.
In the first place, it is hard to disagree with the view of the Secretary
of State that, setting aside for the moment how this role is to be
judged, failure to hand on any awareness that Britain had once been
a world-wide power would be an extraordinary act of national amne-
sia. It would make much of the rest of Britain's national political
history incomprehensible. For the twentieth century, for instance,
it would be very hard to understand why Britain went to war in
1914 and impossible to follow much of the course of the British
war effort between 1939 and 1945 without some understanding of
British interests outside Europe. Young people in the later 1990s
will no doubt be living in a Britain that is merging ever more
closely with the rest of Europe. They would, however, have a
very misleading impression of the past if they thought that the
path to Europe had been smooth or that, because of their deep
involvement in empire or Commonwealth, previous generations of
British people had regarded that destination as the inevitable or even
as a desirable outcome. However tightly integrated into Europe it

may then be, Britain in the 1990s is also likely to be a member of the Commonwealth. It would be an impoverishment if young British people came to regard citizens of other Commonwealth countries as wholly alien to them; in any case, it is highly likely that Hong Kong and South Africa will continue to provide sharp reminders of the imperial past.

Total ignorance of the history of empire would also seriously impair understanding of British economic and social history. 'I do not see how one can understand the nature of the British "nation" outside of the imperial and post-imperial experience', Shula Marks has recently argued, concluding her essay with a plea for what is in a sense a British-directed study of empire: 'Third World historians are beginning to show what empire has meant to them. British historians have largely failed to ask what empire has done to "us"'.[5] Links between empire and economy and society at home have in fact been explored from a number of points of view, but in general with most pertinacity from the left. They are the staple of the analyses of 'imperialism' begun in the work of J.A. Hobson. They are a major theme of Eric Williams's *Capitalism and Slavery* of 1944 and of Peter Fryer's *Black People in the British Empire: an Introduction* written in the same tradition in 1988. Not surprisingly, there is no agreement about the extent of the imperial input into the British economy or about the degree to which society and institutions were shaped by the imperial experience. Influence in certain areas is, however, beyond controversy. Bristol, Liverpool and Glasgow rose to opulence in the eighteenth century to a large extent on African, Caribbean and North American trade. In the late nineteenth century India became the largest single market for British exports, particularly for Lancashire cotton cloth. What can legitimately be regarded as an 'imperial' strand in British culture can be identified over a long period from the mid-nineteenth to the mid-twentieth centuries, although there is much debate about its extent and even about its particular manifestations.[6]

To regard empire as something exogenous to the main currents of British history, an interest of only an élite minority, now to be treated with disdain or even with ridicule would be profoundly unhistorical. Noel Coward's 'Mad dogs and Englishmen' was no doubt a salutary piece of satire in its time, but it and similar pieces may give a misleading impression about the commitment of great sections of British society to empire as late as the 1950s. In a collection which explores for schools in the London borough of Haringey what she calls *Connections* between their locality and the world, Sylvia Collicott convincingly argues for the centrality of the experience of empire: 'Everybody in Britain was affected by the growth of mercantilism and empire, be it by drinking Lipton's tea, sporting an Indian paisley pattern or by developing and endorsing racist views. Local people have always been part of the process of imperialism'.[7] The purpose of Ms Collicott's collection is to take the study of the British imperial experience beyond its role as an integral part of British history and to use it to link local, national and world history, through demonstrating what she calls 'the two-way passage of peoples and ideas'.[8]

There are obvious dangers, of which Ms Collicott is very well aware, in using the empire as a link in this way. In its Final Report, the History Working Group stressed the importance of the study of 'countries and societies from their own perspective' in order to 'help pupils to appreciate the diversity of human society'. This is a widely-supported objective and it can reasonably be argued that empire is potentially a distorting and Anglo-centric focus through which to see societies whose histories should be studied in their own right. Insensitive teaching could of course produce those distortions, but, skilfully presented, the huge wealth of recorded and remembered experience embodied in the history of British imperial expansion is an invaluable resource for creatively illuminating world history. For many individual families memories of the experience are likely to be both vivid and very varied indeed. The empire involved huge movements of people: some, like slaves, indentured labourers or convicts, relatively well written about; others not yet so systematically studied, such as the waves of migration to Australia or Canada, the transfer of some of the very poorest of British society to be soldiers in imperial garrisons or immigration into Britain from the Commonwealth. At a more abstract level, appropriate for fourteen to sixteen-year-olds, the theme of empire further links British to world history. Without a knowledge of the colonial legacy that goes beyond a caricature, patterns of political and economic evolution in much of the contemporary world are hard to understand.

The intellectual case for the serious study of empire in a national curriculum thus seems to be a strong one; but this does not necessarily dispose of practical objections. Can the issues be made comprehensible to pupils at school and be presented at that level within a framework of judgement that will not be socially divisive? Other things being equal, the controversial nature of a topic enhances rather than detracts from its value for teaching history. At the outset the History Working Group was reminded of the provisions of the Education (No 2) Act of 1986 that prohibits 'political indoctrination' and 'requires balanced presentation of opposing views'. It fully endorses the need to ensure that history teaching shall not be used for 'indoctrination or social engineering'. To achieve this end it recommends that there should be what is called an attainment target to test pupils' 'increased awareness of different interpretations and points of view about the past'. The history of empire, which has aroused so much passion, would seem to be an admirable vehicle for teaching pupils to understand conflicting points of view.

So indeed it is. But some of the implications of the conflicting points of view need also to be considered. There can be no doubt whatsoever that for most of the first half of the twentieth century much British school education on the subject of the empire was intended precisely to be indoctrination and social engineering. As has very frequently been pointed out, much of the rhetoric of public schools (to which pupils may or may not have been resistant) was stridently imperialistic. Awareness of empire and pride in it was consciously incorporated into syllabuses for elementary schools.[9] Overtly pro-empire text-books remained in common use in British schools until well after the Second World War. By the end of their shelf life, some of the sentiments in these books no doubt looked more than a little dated and were not necessarily being taken very seriously either by teachers or by pupils. But the point can reasonably be made that it was not specific statements in particular books that were significant, so much as implied assumptions. It has been alleged that an 'imperial curriculum' was until relatively recently taught in many British schools[10] and there is some foundation for this. Implied assumptions, according to a distinguished historian of education, included beliefs in 'British technological, cultural, financial, constitutional, legal, moral and religious superiority' and that 'the peoples of the empire were largely contented with their increasing prosperity and appreciative of British order, justice and fair play' which was guiding them in due time towards autonomous membership of the Commonwealth.[11] In short, from the 1920s onwards the emphasis seems to have shifted from portraying the empire as a source of power to stressing an empire held together by British benevolence.

Recent academic history has not been very supportive of ideas of the empire as benevolence. Not perhaps surprisingly, calculations of British national interest have been clearly detected in the transformation from empire to Commonwealth or in such schemes of colonial 'development' as were launched. The effects of colonial education or, in the light of contemporary environmental concerns, of colonial public works, now often look much more equivocal than they once did. The Commonwealth alliance realistically has to be seen like other alliances, often to have involved acute conflicts of interest, as for instance over the deployment of Australian troops in both world wars. It would, however, be an exceptionally churlish and ultimately inadequate historian who can find nothing to admire about the lives of many people involved in empire or who will not take account of the idealism and loyalty that it could evoke, not only in Britain.

Although relics of an 'imperial curriculum', and the assumptions of superiority on which they rest, may be withering, it is widely held that they are not withering fast enough, especially in a society whose ethnic composition has changed significantly since 1945. 'The essential racism of the official version of our history', writes Peter Fryer, 'is seen above all in its glorification of the British empire and its arrogant attitude to those who were the empire's subjects.'[12] In a persuasive and subtle analysis Paul Rich has argued that, in its later stages, imperial ideology, with its ideals of paternalist benevolence, may have actually hindered the spread in Britain of pseudo-scientific racism, but that this 'imperialism, even its late and relatively benign phase, perpetuated a climate of opinion in Britain well into the twentieth century that buttressed a set of social models based upon a hierarchy of races, with the white Anglo-Saxons at the top'. 'Imperial conceptualising', he concludes, still remains a potent force.[13] In 1985 the Swann Report, *Education for All*, criticised the survival of what it termed anachronistic views of the world and recommended that racism in schools or elsewhere be identified and countered. Those who seek to promote multi-cultural education generally do not advocate that the history of the empire should be ignored (a recent book has felt it necessary to print a list of territories once ruled by Britain, since 'many people including many teachers are not aware of the full extent of the British empire'[14]), but imply that it should be taught in a 'positive' way to dispel stereotypes or Anglo-centric views.

The History Working Group has strongly endorsed the contribution that history can make to the objectives of multi-cultural education. 'The historical skills that pupils should acquire, such as advancing reasoned arguments, and taking account of a range of views, should assist in identifying, and thus combating, racial and other forms of prejudice and stereotypical thinking.' While the Group could perhaps be accused of not proposing a positive counter-programme to any relics of the 'imperial curriculum', teachers are free to do so; no attempt is of course made to prescribe the interpretation which teachers may wish to apply to the suggested topics, provided that they show a proper regard to the attainment targets' insistence on historical understanding, awareness of possible alternative interpretations and respect for evidence.

The Group's strict adherence to its own rules against prescribing interpretations has, however, exposed it to some misunderstanding. In the key stage three unit on the history of the empire the group chose as an option one of the most widely debated episodes in the history of British expansion, the South African War of 1899-1902, and suggested that it might be studied through three highly controversial figures, Rhodes, Kruger and Milner. In trying to make up their minds about this episode and the roles of these people, pupils would be engaged with issues that deeply divided contemporaries and that raise fundamental questions about the use and abuse of power. Yet in some press discussion of the curriculum these choices appear to have been interpreted as an attempt to affirm some kind of 'imperial' values.[15]

Such interpretations suggest that many people still have difficulty in seeing the imperial past except in very crude terms of praise and blame. It is not difficult to see why this should be so. Exponents of multi-cultural education have very understandable worries that the old Adam of belief in superiority is not dead. What is at stake on the other side? It is hard to believe that self-esteem about the imperial past has much relation to a British sense of national identity. Conscious imperialism has long been abandoned by the political parties. Arguments that imperial nostalgia rather than a narrower nationalism reasserted itself in the Falklands War in 1982 do not seem very plausible. Nevertheless, for reasons that do not necessarily involve an unhealthy yearning for past 'greatness', it is likely that a considerable number of people, no doubt mostly middle-aged or above, would still resent what they might regard as the systematic denigration of the whole of the British imperial past.

One solution to contentious and potentially divisive issues is to shelve them, concentrating perhaps on less abrasive subjects, like the evolution of the Commonwealth. The price of that would be high in terms of lost historical understanding, both of British and of world history, and of the opportunity to study a phenomenon which has affected so many of the elements of the population of modern Britain, however different its effects on them may have been. The author's personal impression is, for instance, that a number of British people of South Asian origin value the history of British India as a past which they share with many other British people. Another solution is to give teachers freedom to interpret the imperial past from a variety of points of view within such ground rules of respect for evidence and the integrity of historical inquiry, as are laid down in the attainment targets proposed by the Working Group. A consensus view of the empire will not of course emerge from this process. There can be no authorised version, no final casting of the balance sheet of empire. Some antagonisms may be generated. It would, however, be a sign of the maturity of British society if young British people could learn to look at the imperial past as an historical problem to be judged like other problems, rather than one which evokes automatic and unthinking affirmations of loyalty or rejection. The Working Group has throughout its report stressed the value of history in teaching 'that there are no monopolies of the truth'. It is hard to think of many areas of the national past that more need such an approach than the history of the British imperial experience.

NOTES

1. D. Fieldhouse, 'Can Humpty Dumpty be put together again? Imperial history in the 1980s', *Journal of Imperial and Commonwealth History*, XII (1984), 19.

2. See eg P.K.O'Brien, 'The costs and benefits of British imperialism, 1846-1914', *Past and Present*, CXX (1988), 163-200; Paul Kennedy and P.K.O'Brien, 'Debate', ibid., CXXV (1989), 186-99; Andrew Porter, 'The balance sheet of empire', *Historical Journal*, XXXI (1988), 685-99.

3. 'History, the nation and empire: sniping from the periphery', *History Workshop*, XXIX (1990), 112.

4. R. Ritchie, ed, *Enoch Powell: A Nation or No Nation* (1978), p 67.

5. *History Workshop*, p 117.

6. For what might be regarded as a maximal statement of the case for a strong imperial strand, see the series of *Studies in Imperialism*, ed by John M. MacKenzie for the Manchester University Press, especially, *Imperialism and Popular Culture*, John M. MacKenzie ed. (1986).

7. *Connections, Haringey: Local-National-World Links* (1986). p 112.

8. 'What should we teach in primary schools?', *History Workshop*, XXIX (1990), 110.

9. Pamela Horn, 'English elementary education and the growth of the imperial ideal', *Benefits bestowed? Education and British Imperialism* ed. J.A. Mangan, (1988), pp 39-55.

10. S. Tomlinson, *Multi-cultural Education in White Schools* (1990), p 72.

11. Richard Aldrich, 'Imperialism in the study and teaching of history', *Benefits bestowed?*, p 30.

12. *Black People in the British Empire: An Introduction* (1988), p xiii.

13. *Race and Empire in British Politics* (1985), pp 5, 204, 209.

14. Tomlinson, *Multi-cultural Education*, pp 85-6.

15. See reports in *Times*, 30 March 1990, *Times Education Supplement*, 30 March 1990 and especially Judith Judd in *The Independent on Sunday*, 1 April 1990, an imaginative piece of writing that does not seem to have been based on a reading of the report.

JOHN MORRILL

"The historian does not analyse a still photograph; he analyses a rather chewed up and faded cine-film. The resulting sense of trajectory, of the momentum behind particular lines of historical development, is surely one we all need."

THE NATIONAL CURRICULUM debate has all the hallmarks of the most arid disputations of scholastic theologians. In the struggle to define forms, we lose sight of ends: in the contestation over *what* history should be taught, we have lost sight of *why* it should be taught: and in so far as there has been a discussion of *why* it should be taught, it has been the *whys* of the educationalist not the *whys* of the historian that have been debated. I will offer a few thoughts on the debate as it has unfolded to date, and then suggest how a concern with the purpose of historical study as understood by the historian should both strengthen the case for history as a foundation subject and clarify the debate about what should be taught.

Approaching the final report of the History Working Group as a father of four school-age children, as an academic historian long employed by an Examining Board to design syllabuses and award grades at eighteen plus, and as one who spends a lot of time in schools wrestling to introduce GCSE, I have formed some clear personal views on what has been happening. I have no doubt that there has been a great heat generated as a result of a simple confusion (or perhaps conflation) of history as a class-room experience and history as an examined subject. My overwhelming impression is that the class-room experience of history has been enormously enhanced by the kind of thinking that is encapsulated in GCSE and that underlies the report of the Working Group. Against the new scholasticism of the school syllabus of the previous generation (the absorption of an interpretation of the past through textbooks that are digests of the best commentaries upon the commentaries of the Masters), has come a new humanism (back to the primary sources, with all the limiting of *sweep* that involves, and with all the dangers of loss of perspective but with a new emphasis on personal discovery and on the imaginative recreation of mental worlds of past times). The benefits – across the ability range – seem to me palpably to outweigh the losses. The identification of different skills which can be emphasized (spotlighted, not filtered out) in different teaching exercises is possible and desirable. What has gone wrong is that when we come to examine those GCSE syllabuses we create tests that quite speciously seek to do what no practising historian would ever do, and which no citizen with historical understanding will ever do again. We separate out ('disaggregate' is the jargon word: I prefer 'dis-integrate') the various mental activities of the historian. It is at this point that the 'skills *vs* content' debate becomes a live issue. If we recognize that the concern with what is taught (or more properly, what is learnt) needs to be separated from how what has been learnt is examined, then in my view we have gone a long way to solving the problem. As far as national curriculum history is concerned, this removes much of the anxiety. For there will be no assessment of history at the end of the key stages. Of course, we are left with a debate about the wisdom of so much prescription of particular epochs at particular ages (if I was an Anglo-Saxon historian I would be cross to see my subject restricted to nine-year olds). I would much rather the national curriculum had been set with a looser set of criteria, and with merely prescribing a healthy balance of local, British, European and extra-European history, and of recent and remoter periods, and leaving particular choices to the enthusiasms, resources and cultural imperatives of particular schools. But in the real world, I accept that if the Working Group had not been prescriptive about content, then a handful of publishers would have been. For nothing is clearer than that the *real* syllabuses will be determined by the integrated five-sixteen course units now being evolved by those publishers.

Historical skills are means to an end; not an end in themselves. The debate about history in the school curriculum often seems to be conducted as though the reason for studying history were either the acquisition of a body of knowledge or the development of a job lot of skills. Both of these are, however, subordinate to an overriding purpose: the acquisition of a greater understanding of the world we live in.

Political, social, cultural institutions of particular times and places, and the value systems prevailing in particular times and places, can only be understood by the application of what I will call *historical logic*. This is best explained by an analogy. When I was an undergraduate, I was introduced to the pleasures of solera madeira (a solera 1862 as it happens). Every year after 1862, part of a vat of wine was drawn off, and new wine added to fill up the cask. The wine drawn off each year is thus always developing and changing as the older vintage matures and as the young wine adds its own distinctive flavour; and although the volume of original wine becomes smaller and smaller, yet always some molecules will remain and will help to give distinctiveness. The wine added in some years may be especially dominant; and the addition of sour wine would be ineradicable.

I find this a very helpful way of looking at historical processes. Many of the characteristic institutions and cultural values of particular communities derive from cumulative historical experience. No one would or could ever sit down and design the University of Cambridge. The only logic it possesses that explains the relationship of the colleges to one another and to 'the university' is an historical logic. Once one is aware of its origins as a guild of independent masters of arts (precisely paralleling the guilds of independent merchants or cobblers or butchers) binding themselves together to protect their art and to maintain standards and taking their own apprentices in learning, one can begin to see how it has continuously evolved; even though the dominant flavours are those of more recent vintages, especially late Victorian and post-war ones. Similarly the historian of the British parliament will be able to explain its particular characteristics best by noticing that (as much by chance as design) the medieval Commons sat in a chapel with antiphonal seating inducing a particular form of confrontational politics; and by examining the tension throughout its history between Parliament as a branch of the *curia regis* and as a High Court. Thus for all the filtering and evolutionary force of past centuries, it is easier to explain why and how such institutions exist and function in terms of historical process than by any other form of analysis or conceptualisation. The historian does not analyse a still photograph; he analyses a rather chewed up and faded cine-film. The resulting sense of trajectory, of the momentum behind particular lines of historical development, is surely one we all need.

Why is Britain still a monarchy? Any analysis will show that as the power of the state has evolved over the centuries, so the discretion of the Head of State has been more and more circumscribed. One powerful argument in favour of monarchy, indeed, is precisely the culmination (in a historically-logical sense) of that process: an English monarchy which is less important for the power that it enjoys than for the power it denies to others. On the other hand, in strong comparison to the latter, any comparison between English and American history will show how, in the former attempts to achieve limits on executive tyranny have never been matched by effective checks on legislative tyranny. In my analogy with solera madeira, I pointed out that the introduction of sour wine would leave an ineradicable taste for ever. One could develop that simile in relation to the Cromwellian and Williamite years of Irish history, though at a deeper level of analysis, one would want to know why the scars caused by the 1100 years of successive waves of invaders and conquerors of England up to the Norman Conquest healed so much better than the successive invasions of Ireland from mainland Britain.

The inculcation of a sense of historical logic, and of the processes of erosion (the erosion caused by centuries of relentless but calm pressure; the erosion brought on by the occasional hurricane and tidal wave) is the first and foremost benefit from the study of history, and it can be adapted to all ages and circumstances. It can begin with local history, with the development of a parish church, the rise and fall of a mill or mine, the changes in a local landscape or townscape, and move outwards towards an understanding of a national culture and its institutions and towards the value-systems and developments of many other civilizations. An ancillary purpose to any study of history, indeed, is the development of respect for a range of other historical communities and how they had made sense of their world. Such a study ought to inculcate a greater respect for those with different value-systems (as being different and not superior) and a greater humility about the achievements of our own situation in time and space.

But the greatest lesson is to deepen our sense of ourselves in time. The great danger of this enterprise is what has been called 'Whig' history, too often, but wrongly, assumed to be synonymous with a teleological view of the past. There are great dangers of distorting the past by a preoccupation with seeking out and highlighting the roots of the present in that past. But we must not confuse teleology with anachronism. As Glenn Burgess has recently written, we need to distinguish between [a] history written as the story of how the present came to be what it is ('weak' teleology, and not necessarily involving anachronism); and [b] the use of present-day categories to organize our accounts of the past ('strong' teleology, which is anachronistic).[1]

The task of the historian then, is to tell a story which has an end (*telos*), but which respects the integrity of the events it narrates. The historians must work with the might-have-beens of that past, with its open-endedness, as much as with its outcome, an outcome appropriate to that time, not to ours. The historian explaining why a civil war broke out in 1642 is being teleological whether or not he or she concludes it was inevitable: it happened and its unexpectedness as a happening is as much a statement of outcome as an account that purports to show that a discredited system of government had been in the process of disintegration for some decades. Both explanations are teleological by their essence; but neither is false history unless it imports modern categories and value systems into its account of the collapse of royal authority.

If historians (and here I mean all those who study the past, at whatever age) are to respect the integrity of the past that they study, they must adopt what I will call both the vertical and the horizontal approaches to the subject. 'Vertical history' (I think the term was coined by Patrick Collinson about denominational historians writing the history of their own Christian church or sect) is that which discards the dross of the particular and contingent – the prejudices, blindnesses and contentious of the age – in order to extract the residual gold, the truth and insight of enduring value. In intellectual history this is the history of an idea – natural rights, for example, or (an intellectual equivalent of the search for the source of the Nile) the moment at which the language of liberties turns into a concern with Liberty. In ecclesiastical history it is the search for a core of denominational testimony; in political history the birth of party or similar exercises in scholarly embryology. 'Horizontal' history resolutely sets out to place each event, idea, institution into its contemporary context. It seeks out not the enduring, the survival of the fittest idea, but rather the contingent and the ordinary in the context of the time. The 'vertical' approach emphasizes the continuity of past and present; the 'horizontal' approach, as William Lamont has it, 'can serve best by restoring a sense of inaccessibility. The world where the King is equated with God and the Pope with Antichrist; where witches fly in the night and women give birth to monsters; where Jesuits peddle lies and the Apocalypse conveys truths – this is not what S.R. Gardiner had in mind when he wrote of the "Puritan Revolution". But this is the world of the seventeenth-century puritan.'[2] It is by combining the two approaches that we avoid the nominalism of extreme revisionism and the anachronism of Whig history. In combining them we create an agenda that creates an essential part of every child's and every citizen's education. The past existed and it still exists, most tangibly in the traces of itself that survive in its documentary remains and artefacts. The task of the historian is that of a radio receiver, to pick up and to amplify the often distorted messages from the past without adding its own distortions or limiting those messages through clumsy filtering. The training in the arts of the historian allows us all to understand ourselves in time, and to accept humbly the limits and relativity of our own understanding of ourselves. In achieving that, then, all those who study history need to recognize its central purpose: to seek out the past in the present, and not the present in the past.

NOTES

1. *Historical Journal,* xxxii, no 3 (1990).
2. W. Lamont, *Richard Baxter and the Millenium* (1981), pp 22-4.

MICHAEL HUNTER

"We ought to be able to reconstruct the real past imaginatively enough to render embroidered versions superfluous, and, if necessary, we must find means of showing why it is better to know about what actually occurred than about a cosmetic substitute."

As the debate over history's place in the National Curriculum rages, I write as one rather remote from school history. In part, this is because my research mainly concerns topics that are rarely taught in schools, particularly the history of science – though this is something which should perhaps change. Secondly, I teach in an institution – Birkbeck College at the University of London – where our undergraduates are mature students, usually a decade or more away from their school days, whose acquaintance with history therefore tends to owe as much to general reading and experience as to what they learnt in the classroom. My views about the role of history are also affected by my involvement in historical conservation, where the past and the present have a direct contact in the real world. For one thing, I have been involved from a preservationist point of view in debates over the current proposals for the redevelopment of King's Cross in central London. I have also collaborated in a book-length study re-evaluating current knowledge of the stone circle at Avebury in Wiltshire in the light of newly discovered early records: this has implications for the management of this internationally important monument. What reflections do these experiences stimulate concerning the place of scholarship and historical understanding in contemporary affairs?

The central fact – at once a dilemma and an opportunity - is that history is both popular and academic. This raises questions about what the proper relationship between the two should be. Hardly a day passes without a newspaper report about some new venture exploiting or commercialising the past, and books popularising historical subjects often reach the best-seller lists. Yet at the same time, the study of the past is rightly academic. Historians and other cognate specialists, both academics in related disciplines like archaeology and scholars in institutions like museums, represent the centre of the subject: it is they who set its agenda and advance its boundaries, in a way which is different from a profession like architecture, where the teachers are at one remove from the practitioners.

Perhaps partly because of this, it is easy for university historians, surrounded by students moulded in their own image, to forget – or to fail to notice – the distance that separates their view of their subject from that of the general public. This is perhaps most easily observed in any bookshop or library, where, in contrast to the scholar's presumption that the authorship of historical works is all important, most enquirers look for or remember books according to the topics covered rather than the author dealing with them. This encapsulates a quite different view of the subject. Moreover, exposure to academic history for those fresh from a 'normal' background can come as something of a shock. This was well-expressed in execrable verse by a former student of mine at Birkbeck College, who wrote:

It isn't, I find, the *facts* that people try to get clearly seen,
It's what historians think of what historians think they mean.

What makes things worse are recent developments within historical study which increase the distance between scholars and the public. The problem is exemplified by certain emanations of the trend in historical study known as 'revisionism'. In itself, the revision of accepted historical wisdom is something of which I am very much in favour; but historians need to be more alert than they sometimes are to the broad context of what they are doing. A sense of perspective is needed to ensure that undue significance is not attached to revision for its own sake, and this has been lacking, for instance, in some of the more recondite of recent studies of early Stuart politics. It is also disappointing that, although some of the revisionist work on this period has been based on local studies, it has rarely tapped the genuine popular interest that exists in local history.

A more worrying trend, to be seen particularly in ancillary fields like art history and the history of science, is the introduction of fresh (and, it may often be felt, inappropriate) theoretical models into history as a means of reinterpretating data from the past. This has been particularly noticeable in my own field of the history of science, and not least in studies of English science in the late seventeenth and early eighteenth centuries. Here, a good deal of sociological jargon has come into play, including concepts like 'discourse', 'experimental space', and 'literary technology', often denoting phenomena which could be much more simply described.

An example of this is provided by the use of the word 'institutionalisation', as seen in the context of the establishment of the new experimental science of the late seventeenth and early eighteenth centuries. To me – and, I would have thought, to most people – the world relates to what it sounds as if it relates to, namely the setting up of scientific and other institutions, most famously the Royal Society, founded in 1660. But it turns out that sociologists use it in a completely different sense, to mean the establishment of collective norms ('the processes by which knowledge and associated behaviours are established as the basis for standardized collective reference and action', in the succinct words of one recent commentator on the science of the period).

It seems to me that such trends in the study of the subject are scholastic in the worst sense, tending to invest topics which in themselves are quite accessible to the general reader with an unnecessary technical mystique. Though this may excite young graduate students weaned on such study, who have never known anything else, it puts my own students right off. Indeed, here we need to learn from the academic discipline where, sadly, this problem is perhaps at its most acute, English Literature. Ironically, this is a study which above all others ought to be accessible to the general public, which yet is in danger of becoming one of the most repellent through the adoption of a theory-laden, jargon-ridden agenda.

In fact, it could be claimed that the problems of communication between experts and the public are bad without making them worse. Even the detail which historical study inevitably entails could be seen as problematic, particularly the ever greater complexity of modern interpretation. But against this various things can be said. One is that detail is not in itself necessarily unpopular, so long as it is detail of the right kind. As the success of books like Le Roy Ladurie's *Montaillou* or Schama's *Citizens* shows, a detailed depiction of life in past periods can catch the public imagination: the trend in historical study christened by Lawrence Stone 'the revival of narrative' is clearly itself a belated recognition of this fact.

In addition, if the past *is* complicated, we surely do not need to apologise for doing justice to this. There is no reason why academic historians' response to the challenge of popularisation should be to abandon standards and rush for the lowest common denominator. Much in the current exploitation of popular interest in the past is trivialising, if not downright false, and it is important that this should be publicly stated. A case in point is provided by some of the activities and a good deal of the promotion indulged in by the more opportunistic owners of country houses – ranging from waxworks, jousting and feasting to unsubstantiated claims for royal visits to their houses.

As the public become more familiar with the products of historical popularisation, they need to be helped to be more discriminating and to be able to distinguish the true from the fake. There are lessons to be learnt from Maggie Smith's memorable performance as an improvising tour-guide in the first act of Peter Schaffer's *Lettice and Lovage* which the historical profession has not yet absorbed. We ought to be able to reconstruct the real past imaginatively enough to render embroidered versions superfluous, and, if necessary, we must find means of showing why it is better to know about what actually occurred than about a cosmetic substitute.

What, therefore, should be our agenda? The first thing to be stressed is that there is curiosity about history at all levels, and that the current popularisation undoubtedly has a spin-off effect at a more advanced level, from extra-mural classes to degree programmes. As the current Admissions Tutor for History at Birkbeck College, and hence catering for mature students seeking to do a B.A., I can vouch for the fact that interest in degree-level history among the public is higher than ever. This is something to be taken advantage of. It is also striking how much of an appetite there is among such students for quite traditional subjects of historical study, of which historians have no need to feel ashamed.

We should also emphasise the value of historical study both in its own right and as a social skill in modern society. As an obsessive, instinctive historian since childhood, there have been times when I have felt slightly embarrassed by my interest and anxious to proclaim my allegiance to the 'relevance' of the social sciences. Now, on the contrary, I revel in the fullness of history and the emptiness of its jargon-ridden academic rivals. Historians are prone to underestimate the value of what they do. It may be argued that one of the most useful intellectual skills which it is possible to teach is historical-mindedness, with the attendant critical attitude towards contemporary issues that this induces. Everything has a history, and our understanding of almost any matter is enhanced by being able to place it in its historical context. This also encourages a healthy general sense of the degree to which human experience is relative.

In addition, historians tend to underestimate the skills which they possess and which they pass on to their students. The techniques of historical analysis are many and complex, ranging from the ability to read antiquated handwriting to an acute sense of historical context which makes it possible to assess the value of different sources, and a sense of responsibility to ensure that no crucial information has been overlooked. Yet in general we teach such analysis almost by a kind of osmosis, testing it by criticising its absence in a piecemeal way and taking it for granted once it is in place. In the course of my recent work on the early records of Avebury, which was done in collaboration with non-historians, I became more than usually aware of the skills that I possessed and with which they were unfamiliar. This came to a climax when we decided to edit a complex eighteenth-century text, with multiple levels of rewriting and revision which needed to be intelligibly presented to the reader. In preparing this, I was reminded of the degree of expertise which I brought to bear on the task which could almost only be defined negatively – one knew what was wrong when it was missing, but would have difficulty in a positive definition of it. We need to be more self-conscious in identifying and proclaiming these techniques than we are at present: what seems obvious to us as historians may seem less so to others than we realise.

Moreover, these skills have a direct relevance to current debates, for instance those on conservation in which I have been involved. At Avebury, pure scholarship was needed. It turned out that current interpretation – and management – of the site had been based on ignorance of crucial evidence even about key parts of the antiquity like the 'Cov' at the centre of the northern inner circle: this derived from the observations of early antiquarians who saw stones in place which have since been destroyed. In addition, sensitive, historically-alert study was required in order satisfactorily to assess the relative reliability of different early records.

A further – perhaps more surprising – example of the need for scholarly attitudes may be taken from the King's Cross area. At the heart of the current redevelopment site there is a group of buildings which represents the almost complete survival of a goods-handling complex established when the Great Northern Railway came to London in the early 1850s. As such, it is a key part of our national heritage, and it is clearly important that great care is taken in deciding which buildings are integral to the group and which are peripheral. What is needed is an essentially scholarly exercise of appraisal, involving an understanding of the historical growth of the complex, the functions of the different buildings and their interrelationship. Yet this is a message which is surprisingly hard to get across to developers prone to take a rather tokenistic attitude to conservation and to think in terms of individual buildings rather than of the group as a whole.

The other thing that historians arguably underestimate is what might be called the power of discovery. When a hitherto-unknown masterpiece by Titian or Gainsborough comes to light, the public loves it; and archaeology, too, has capitalised on the public's curiosity about new and unexpected finds. Why do we not make more of the historical equivalent? I have had various experiences of this recently, which have made me conscious that far more could be achieved in this direction than is currently the case, even if we are inevitably dependent for such publicity on the slightly capricious patronage of journalists and television producers. With the discoveries concerning Avebury that I have already referred to, the general fascination with archaeology makes it far from surprising that a considerable amount of coverage was given to the new documents whose discovery began the exercise of reinterpretation in which I have been involved. At one point I appeared on ITN's *News at Ten*, and even the mechanic who repairs my motorcycle had seen me talking about 'Druid stones' (an interesting example, incidentally, of the failure to oust a popular view of the origin of megaliths which has been discredited among scholars for over a century). I had an equally telling experience a couple of years ago with the discovery of a hitherto unknown seventeenth-century diary, that of Samuel Jeake of Rye, which I published (in conjunction with Annabel Gregory) as *An Astrological Diary of the Seventeenth Century*. This inspired a full-page feature in the *Hampstead and Highgate Express* (my local paper), comparable coverage in the Brighton *Evening Argus* and an interview on Radio Sussex. Jeake is not quite Pepys, but there was a real sense of a new historical personality being born, and new texts are potentially as exciting as new prehistoric monuments.

Moreover this is where the emphasis in reinterpretation should lie. Returning to what I said earlier about the dangers of a dry scholasticism, what we *need* is re-evaluation based on new evidence, rather than new theory. Arguably the most exciting of historical research consists of luminous new insights of this kind. Consider, for instance, the extraordinary story of the Lesbian nun, Benedetta Carlini, revealed from documents in the State Archive at Florence by Judith Brown in her book, *Immodest Acts*, and providing a window not only into the history of sexuality but also into early modern religious life. It is work like this that is historically most exciting: at the same time, it also best illustrates the *point* of scholarly research.

This raises all kinds of questions about historical interpretation. Underlying the public's curiosity about such 'discoveries' is a rather old-fashioned idea of history, a belief that when all the facts are known a wholly objective view of the past will exist. Historians would differ: they, by contrast, are aware of the extent to which historical interpretation is a constantly shifting artefact, and that discoveries often stem from curiosity about new questions. But this is only another example of historians taking themselves for granted, underestimating the role that their skills and knowledge give them in a public domain dominated by a new enthusiasm for history. We need to be sensitive to the problems of access and communication; but we also need to exploit and build on the positive contribution to culture and understanding which history could and should be making. It is a real challenge for the 1990s.

ALICE PROCHASKA

"[Students] must 'realize that true patriotism celebrates the great moral force of the American idea as a nation that unites as one people the descendants of many cultures, races, religions and ethnic groups. The American story is unfinished, and the outcome rests in the student's hands.' The history curriculum in schools thus assumes a role as part of a great national purpose. "

THE DEBATE OVER history in the curriculum of English and Welsh schools has drawn upon and generated large quantities of print since the passage of the Education Reform Act 1988. The issues that have attracted debate range from pedagogy to politics, to questions of national and local cultures, many of them addressed elsewhere in this book. I would like to devote my contribution to some aspects of the question, why does it matter that people should learn history in school? The answers to this question usually link, sooner or later, with the notion of identity: the identity of the individual, the local community, the social or ethnic group, and then the identity of the nation state within which the individual functions as a citizen. There are two documents, the *Final Reports* of the National Curriculum History Working Group and the History Committee for Wales, which are central to the current national debate and a third, which predates them, is the *History – Social Science Framework* for California public schools, adopted by the California State Board of Education in 1987.

All three documents set out clear, prescriptive recommendations for the teaching of history to school pupils who will learn primarily through the medium of the English language. All three address a perceived need to improve and enhance the teaching of history in schools. And all of them set their work in context by attempting to explain why history is important. The English and Welsh documents, of course, are conditioned by a legislative framework and clear governmental guidelines within which their authors had to work. They possess the unusual quality that their recommendations (or some of them, but the authors cannot control which) are liable to become law. In the Californian case the *Framework* is not compulsory and arose out of quite different political circumstances within a very different educational system. It is nevertheless intended to be adopted as the norm for teaching history and the social sciences in Californian schools. It also addresses the whole area of the social sciences which, however, are clearly seen as being led, if not dominated, by history. Some comparisons may be valid, therefore. In particular, there are subtle differences in the ways in which the three documents confront the question of national and personal identity, and the connection of each type of identity to learning history.

The Californian *Framework* is introduced by the authors writing personally, with clear assertions of their stance. 'As Educators we have the responsibility of preparing these children for the challenges of living in a fast-changing society.' Then:

> As educators in the field of history – social science, we want our students to perceive the complexity of social, economic, and political problems. We want them to have the ability to differentiate between what is important and what is unimportant. We want them to know their rights and responsibilities as American citizens. We want them to understand the meaning of the Constitution as a social contract . . . We want them to respect the right of others to differ with them. We want them to take an active role as citizens and to know how to work for change . . . We want them to understand the value, the importance, and the fragility of democratic institutions. We want them to realize that only a small fraction of the world's population . . . has been fortunate enough to live under a democratic form of government, and we want them to understand the conditions that encourage democracy to prosper. We want them to develop a keen sense of ethics and citizenship. And we want them to care deeply about the quality of life in their community, their nation and their world.

A later paragraph emphasises the importance of 'ethical understanding', the 'connection between ideas and behavior', and the importance of 'choices made by individuals'. History 'is not simply the ebb and flow of impersonal forces but is shaped and changed by the ideas and actions of individuals and governments'. Finally, the introductory paragraphs conclude with a reference to understanding other parts of the world and the need to 'recognize the political and cultural barriers that divide people as well as the common human qualities that unite them'.

Compare these priorities with those of the English History Working Group (I will refer to it as such because its recommendations apply in their totality only to English schools, although the group included a Welsh representative and worked in consultation with the History Committee for Wales). The 'purposes of school history' are introduced with the somewhat more distant construction, 'We consider that the purposes of school history are', followed by a series of infinitives:

i)   to help understand the present in the context of the past
ii)   to arouse interest in the past
iii)   to help to give pupils a sense of identity
iv)   to help to give pupils an understanding of their own cultural roots and shared inheritance
v)   to contribute to pupils' knowledge and understanding of other countries and other cultures in the modern world
vi)   to train the mind by means of disciplined study
vii)   to introduce pupils to the distinctive methodology of historians
viii) to enrich other areas of the curriculum
ix)   to prepare pupils for adult life.

There is no contradiction between these objectives and those of the History Committee for Wales, but the ordering differs. 'We believe', writes the Welsh committee, 'that the over-riding purpose of history in the school curriculum is to provide pupils, through the acquisition of historical knowledge and understanding, with a map of the past. This will help them to understand the inheritance and identity of their own society and those of other societies.' Further, history 'encourages pupils to develop a sense of the "otherness" of the past and an awareness of the differences between different societies and periods'. It offers 'a sense of time, sequence and chronology'; it contributes to pupils' 'awareness of the different geographical dimensions of human experience'; it 'will help them understand the complexity of past – and therefore also of present – societies and the inter-relationships between different facets of human experience'; it also involves the 'development of skills'.

Thus far the distinctions between the three documents appear remarkably small. There is agreement on the importance of history in training people to live as adults in a democratic, pluralist and tolerant society. In the working out of detail and further extrapolation of some general principles, however, differences of emphasis emerge. The Californian document is clear on the question of national identity. A special section headed 'National Identity' affirms the plurality and multicultural nature of the USA first and foremost, and writes it into the national identity. Students *must* 'understand the American creed as an ideology extolling equality and freedom.' 'Students should learn the radical implications of such phrases as "all men are created equal" and study the historic struggle to extend to all Americans the constitutional guarantees of equality and freedom'. Further, they *must* 'realize that true patriotism celebrates the moral force of the American idea as a nation that unites as one people the descendants of many cultures, races, religions and ethnic groups'. 'The American story is unfinished and the outcome rests in the students' hands.' The history curriculum in schools thus assumes a role as part of a great national purpose.

For the Welsh, the question of national identity in the history curriculum is almost resolved for them by the terms of reference of the History Committee for Wales, which instructed them to produce recommendations for the content of Welsh history in the curriculum and the extent to which Welsh perspectives should influence the wider study of history. Not surprisingly (though in marked contrast to the Californian *Framework* which dwells on the ethnic diversity of its populace) they assert that 'The history of Wales is the history of a distinct people and nation'. They go on to argue that 'The centre of gravity of Welsh history has lain in the social, economic and broad cultural experiences of the people of Wales, rather than in the history of state power, high politics, government and international relationships'. It thus serves as a corrective to any concentration on the history of nation states. History, to the Welsh, appears above all to be an organ of 'cultural transmission', and as such it is a crucial safeguard of Welsh identity. While not denying the pluralism of cultural traditions in Britain and even, to some extent, within Wales itself, the emphasis of the Welsh report is on history as a means of preserving and transmitting a very particular sense of the identity of a people.

The English report seems notably less concerned with national identity than either its Californian or its Welsh counterpart. The brief of the History Working Group was to draw up a report with 'at its core the history of Britain'. It addresses the question of British history as something in which England's role, 'though often dominant, has by no means been exclusive'. Part of the intention of the report is therefore to redress the balance of traditional historiography by drawing attention to the importance of Welsh, Scottish and Irish history in the history of Britain. Thus there is no explicit consideration of 'Englishness' in the report, even though its full recommendations apply only to English schools. The geographical levels at which history ought to be considered jump from the local to the British, and thence to Europe and the world. British history itself, however, 'should be the foundation of the pupils' historical learning, since it is the main framework of their immediate experience in political, economic, social and cultural terms'. This rationale for studying national history is similar in tone to the Californians' for studying Californian history: 'Not only is California [the students'] home; it is a fascinating study in its own right'. The remarkable thing is that the English report, unlike the Californian, contains no higher level of explicit national consciousness. In that respect, the Welsh and Californian reports are closer to each other.

This is not to say that there is no sense of national *purpose* in the English History Working Group's report. On the contrary, in its emphasis on inheritances (plural) and its section on citizenship, as well as in other parts of the report, there is to be found a belief in history as the foundation of personal, social and political identity which is just as clear (even if less boldly stated) as that of the Americans and the Welsh. 'History is a vital element within the curriculum for the education of all citizens. Respect for people of other cultures and from other backgrounds; an informed curiosity about the wider world; an understanding of how rights and liberties develop and how they may be threatened; some comprehension of what individuals can do within society and under the rule of law; all of these must be firmly grounded in an understanding of history.' But it is ultimately a social identity rather than a national one. For some reason, the humane and responsible vision which informs all three reports cannot be couched in national or patriotic terms, in the case of the English/British; whereas neither the Californian-Americans nor the Welsh display any such inhibitions.

Some of the argument in Britain that has surrounded publication of the History Working Group's Final Report has questioned whether history needs to be considered in national terms at all. Some of the best founded criticisms of the report are directed at its relative neglect of European history, a direct consequence of the instructions given to the group to give at least fifty per cent of the curriculum to British history. As the debate broadens and continues, it may be worth considering such questions further. If there is a certain shyness of overt patriotism in the British national debate, does this merely point to an underlying sense of national superiority which people believe that history will reveal without its needing to be stated? Or is there perhaps a sense of shame at aspects of our national past (imperialism, economic decline, industrial exploitation) which inhibits any expression of national pride? Such explanations are not altogether convincing. Meanwhile, although bursting with recommendations for British history, the report explicitly leaves open the interpretations that teachers and pupils alike may make for themselves. And so it invites each individual engaged in the study of history to consider for himself or herself the contribution of self, family, community, locality and nation to the sum of human experience.

ROBERT THORNE

"Professional mistrust of lay enthusiasm, a common enough occurrence at the best of times, has affected architectural historians and conservationists to an unusual extent, perhaps because their expertise is such a recent creation."

AT A TIME WHEN teachers in general feel undervalued it has come as a curious surprise to the historians amongst them to discover what passions their subject can arouse. What is equally remarkable is that in the history curriculum debate there has been a general unanimity in favour of history in schools, with the result that most polemical firepower has been reserved for the question of what should be taught and how. In many ways it must be counted a blessing that the debate has largely been confined to that level, but by becoming a detailed dispute about history in the classroom other perspectives are in danger of being lost sight of. The school curriculum, whether tilted in favour of facts or empathy, shapes the most formal presentation of history that most people receive, yet in countless ways history is also part of their lifetime's experience – memories, images and sounds which infiltrate almost everything they do. Of nothing is that truer than buildings which, seen and used every day, are unavoidable reminders of the past. Such a tangible contact with history, though it may not be part of the classroom timetable, deserves to be more fully taken account of.

Future historians will single out the 1980s as the decade when architecture came onto the agenda as never before. From a glib point of view this will probably be attributed to the Prince of Wales's attacks on contemporary architecture, first in his speech to the RIBA in 1984 and later in his television odyssey and book. His pronouncements have undoubtedly helped to release architectural debate from its professional stranglehold, giving people the courage to voice opinions that they long have held but have been reluctant to articulate. In response to this change the media have adopted architecture as if it was an unheard-of novelty.

Yet the stimulus given to architectural debate by the Prince of Wales would have been ineffective had there been no earlier interest in the subject. Indications of a widespread curiosity about buildings have long been apparent, most of all in the use which people make of their leisure time. As tourist boards repeatedly remind us, trips to historic buildings are one of the most popular forms of family outing – a total of 36.3 million visits in 1988.[1] Even if some go simply for the ride, for others the choice of a country house or a Roman site as the destination is a conscious preference. The same enthusiasm shows itself nearer home in the membership of local amenity societies, which collectively have recruited about a quarter of a million members to the cause of looking after their local architectural environment. From the point of view of many such societies, home improvers are regarded as the worst despoilers yet, like it or not, they too are fascinated by buildings. The money that people put into maintaining their homes, largely through their own efforts, is the most dramatic evidence of all that architecture, broadly considered, has engaged the attention of an immensely wide public: no other spare time activity enjoys such a degree of commitment.[2]

Do-it-yourself enthusiasts and country house visitors are not normally counted as part of the constituency for architecture, though their credentials are often as good as those of many self-proclaimed experts. What characterises the outlook of this wider architectural public is an omnivorous interest in buildings of every kind, an attachment to places which to other eyes may appear valueless, and a generous attitude towards architectural impurities. Above all, amongst home improvers there exists a fascination with the practicalities of construction, and the adaptation of buildings through generations of use. How buildings function seems to them to be as important as what they look like.

It is important to stress these lines of interest because the debate about architecture, even in its most popular forms, has still been conducted in relatively esoteric terms. The failure to acknowledge the extended audience for the subject is particularly true where historic buildings are concerned. Professional mistrust of lay enthusiasm, a common enough occurrence at the best of times, has affected architectural historians and conservationists to an unusual extent, perhaps because their expertise is such a recent creation. Their traditions of thought, though none of them very old, have inhibited their response to alternative viewpoints.

To appreciate how the experts' view of buildings has got out of step with the wider appreciation of them it is necessary to re-examine the recent ancestry of architectural history, and its relationship to conservation policy. In two respects the study of old buildings has as long a pedigree as others kinds of historical scholarship. First, from the Reformation onwards the destruction of buildings has provoked a sentimental reaction, which has acted as an impulse to research and recording. In that respect the recent spate of books on the English country house represents the latest version of a type of writing pioneered in the seventeenth century by studies of monasticism. A second approach to the past, with almost as long an ancestry, has stemmed from architects' interest in earlier styles and techniques. Even in periods of fervent innovation architects have relied on historical experience more than they care to acknowledge. Whenever such dependence has been openly prevalent in architectural practice, as during most of the nineteenth century, architects have looked upon historical research and debate as essential ingredients for successful design.[3]

The common feature of these two traditions, at least until the 1930s, was their unacademic quality. Neither conservation-inspired antiquarians nor working architects regarded the exhaustive study of their topic, and all the documentation relating to it, as being their highest priority: a feeling for picturesque topography, or for the excitements of architectural practice, seemed to be more important. A third way of looking at architecture, normally associated with the German scholar-refugees who arrived in Britain before the Second World War, set these earlier methods to shame by its systematic rigour. Problems of style, attribution and iconography were treated to more precise analysis than before, and local developments were reclassified through international criteria.

The eventual leader of the movement to detach architectural history from its dilettante roots was Nikolaus Pevsner. He settled in London from Göttingen in 1935 with a reputation as an authority on Mannerist and Baroque painting, which turned out to be only an apprenticeship to his study of architecture, especially English architecture in its European context. The other main characteristic of his outlook was his proselytising interest in the virtues of modernism. Had it not in fact happened, it might have seemed wholly improbable that the author of *Pioneers of the Modern Movement from William Morris to Walter Gropius* (1936) was the same person as the chronicler of English architecture, who in the forty-six volumes of the *Buildings of England* (1951-74) almost single-handedly established a gazetteer of amazing thoroughness. Yet on second thoughts it is easy to appreciate that both projects formed part of a single programme, dedicated to describing a sequential view of architecture with its destiny in the most innovative works of the twentieth century. It was partly because of that cohesive sense of direction that Pevsner was able to see the *Buildings of England* finished in his lifetime, but at the cost of imposing a discriminatory view which a generation of users has come to accept as authoritative.

From the earliest volumes onwards what distinguished Pevsner's county by county guides was the assurance with which he sifted the good from the bad, according to a pattern occasionally made bluntly explicit. For instance in his second volume, on Nottinghamshire, his admiration for the furnishings of Egmanton church, as restored in the 1890s, is pulled up short with the judgement that 'as pieces of contemporary art they are of course all valueless', and the Council House in Nottingham is set aside because inferior to Stockholm Town Hall of six years earlier.[4] These and other such evaluations may provoke agreement, fury or just an amused chuckle. Such reactions matter less than the fact that Pevsner, through his established tone, accustomed his public to the idea that architecture was there to be ordered and classified at every turn.

The other architectural historian whose encyclopaedic achievement has been almost as influential is Howard Colvin. From a background as a medieval historian he has revitalised the antiquarian study of architecture by his use of meticulous documentary research. In his *Biographical Dictionary of English Architects 1660-1840* (1954; rev. ed. 1978) attributions are assigned on the basis of tested evidence, with stylistic analogy thrown in only as a last resort. Although starting from a different background and outlook to Pevsner, he too has made his greatest impact as a classifier. Implicit in his emphasis on architectural biography is the assumption that the architect is the key person in the building process, and that buildings produced without the benefit of an architect are of inferior status.

Many other historians have played a part in the coming of age of architectural history since the war – Sir John Summerson and Mark Girouard are the other two names best known to the public – but Pevsner and Colvin have led the way as teachers and writers. The importance of their contribution would be recognised even if their work was known only amongst fellow historians, but their contribution has reached much further – to lay admirers of architecture and, more significantly, to the administrators of building conservation. Partly through their role history and public policy have grown up together, with cross-connections at every stage.

The most familiar aspect of architectural conservation is the protection of buildings through listing – literally the preparation of lists describing and grading buildings of importance area by area. The owner of a designated building has to apply for permission before doing works to it. This process of listing began just after the war, using powers written into the 1944 Planning Act at the insistence of conservation enthusiasts, but it had been talked about much earlier. At the end of the nineteenth century the London County Council had proposed drawing up a register of historic buildings, and circulated forms to local officials and historians for their suggestions ('There are no buildings of historic or architectural interest in Paddington', replied the Vestry Clerk for that area). Nothing came of that survey, but a subsequent LCC initiative in 1937 produced a set of draft lists which were absorbed into the government-organised registers once listing became official policy. The first nationwide cull of buildings for listing was completed in 1968.[5]

In other spheres of government intervention, legislation has generally been the result of a period of lobbying and research.[6] In the case of listing, public concern, increased by anxiety that buildings blighted by wartime treatment might be unknowingly demolished, resulted in government action before the full extent of the question was known. The so-called investigators of historic buildings took to the road in 1946 before Pevsner had tackled his first county, and well before Colvin's masterpiece had appeared. Though they were in no sense starting from scratch, investigators and architectural historians were making their discoveries simultaneously and were feeding information back and forth between each other. All of Pevnser's guides acknowledge the benefit of consulting the official lists, just as investigators referred to Pevsner in places where he had staked out the ground ahead of them. That collaborative spirit was reinforced as students trained by Pevsner, and later by Colvin, became the guardians of historic buildings policy.

The unity of outlook between architectural history and conservation policy has shown itself most explicitly in the criteria laid down for the listing of buildings. The first generation of investigators was equipped with instructions which stated the grounds on which buildings were to be judged: 'The great bulk and staple of the work will deal with clear and undoubted examples of fine building and it may be guessed that numerically the eighteenth century will (in total, though not in all localities) have a clear preponderance over any other'. The kind of building to be given top priority was 'a work of art, the product of a distinct and outstanding mind'; next best were buildings representative of a school of design; and in third place were those composed of 'fragmentary beauties welded together by time and good fortune'. Other criteria really only applied to borderline cases.[7]

Throughout these criteria, and in the lists which resulted, the predominant stress was on the visible quality of buildings. Structural technique is acknowledged but largely through examples where structure is exposed to the eye, such as the Palm House at Kew and the St Pancras train-shed, rather than buildings which hide their structure from view. The virtue of constructional competence, of putting up buildings that will work, is nowhere acknowledged.

And in contentious cases, which until the 1960s included almost all examples of Victorian architecture, exterior excellence had to be backed up by the Colvin-like attribute of a well-known architectural name.

Knowing how they were compiled, it is easy to spot omissions in the lists, just as it is easy to spot buildings which Pevsner missed in his great tour round England. In many instances it is the same buildings which have been overlooked. Pevsner tended to single out ordinary housing only when it was architect-designed or formed part of a specially conceived scheme, and investigators have been encouraged to follow the same priorities for fear of over-filling the lists. Interiors of buildings such as pubs, shops and theatres have fallen foul of the prejudice on both sides in favour of exteriors. Above all, both the lists and the volumes of the *Buildings of England* have been trapped by the way that history is catching up with the present. Pevsner had no difficulty in accommodating the growing interest in Victorian and Edwardian buildings, but found himself increasingly uneasy at the wilful and expressionist tendencies in modern architecture.[8] For their part, the compilers of the lists have been inhibited, sometimes for political reasons, from making a full assessment of the recent past.

Those who first introduce order into a subject can always expect to be chastised for what they have overlooked. What they may not anticipate is the effect of their classification on the understanding of the subject. The alliance between architectural history and the official apparatus for conservation has turned out to be a classic instance of how a particular system, introduced for the best of intentions, can have unforeseen consequences. The process of listing has undoubtedly ensured the salvation of many thousands of buildings which otherwise might have been neglected or destroyed. But its side-effect, like the cumulative effect of Pevsner's guidebook choices, has been to create too blunt a distinction between what is valuable about the past and what is not. It has identified significant cases for special treatment instead of developing a comprehensive view of how to treat buildings of every kind. And by giving primacy to exteriors it has presented only part of the story of architecture as most people know it.

This is not to say that listing should be done away with nor, at the other extreme, that every building put up before (say) 1900 should be given protection. If there is to be a broader understanding of architecture it must start from a different kind of architectural history; one which stresses the construction of buildings and how they are used during their life cycle. It is strange, as Sir John Summerson once remarked, that the study of architecture has been more closely allied to art history than to economic and social history.[9] If other kinds of links had been established in its formative stages something more akin to building history might have emerged, in which matters of style and attribution would have been acknowledged but not given pride of place. There are signs that such an alternative may yet develop. If it does so, the benefits will soon be reflected in a kind of conservation that is both more broad-minded and more realistic.

NOTES

1. *Cultural Trends* 4 (Policy Studies Institute, 1989). This figure does not include visits to churches and cathedrals, estimated as a further 30 million visits a year.
2. *Social Trends* 20 (1990), 162, 168.
3. David Watkin, *The Rise of Architectural History* (1980), Chaps III-IV.
4. Nikolaus Pevsner, *Nottinghamshire* (1951), pp 65-66, 130.
5. Frank Kelsall, 'Listing and the London County Council', ASCHB Transactions, Vol 10 (1983), 48-9; Angus Acworth and Sir Anthony Wagner, '25 Years of Listing', *Architectural Review*, Vol CXLVIII (Nov. 1970), 308-10.
6. Oliver Macdonagh, 'The Nineteenth Century Revolution in Government: A Reappraisal', *Historical Journal*, Vol 1 (1958), 52-67.
7. Ministry of Town and Country Planning, *Instructions to Investigators* (March 1946), pp 9-16.
8. Those responsible for revising the *Buildings of England* have been much more catholic in their tastes. As Pevsner foretold, 'Maybe they long to put in everything they know and can say, maybe a sense of proportion grows slowly' (*Staffordshire*, 1974, p 14).
9. Review of David Watkin (as above), *Architectural Review*, Vol CLXVIII (August 1980), 70.

GORDON MARSDEN

"That medieval world which the Reformation destroyed was one of belief communicated by image. There is a curious sense, as we approach the second millennium, of the wheel come full circle. Perhaps logos and pictures are more easily accommodated than the printed word in the attention span of the three-minute culture."

'TO THE LIVING, to do justice, however belatedly should matter' was the comment offered by that illustrious historian Garrett Mattingly, in his rehabilitation of Philip II's luckless Armada commander, Medina Sidonia. In an appreciation written in the mid 1960s, one of Mattingly's peers, Jack Hexter, astutely pointed out how this phrase illuminates the former's philosophy of history – not, as he wryly observes, that Mattingly ever expounded it 'in ponderous pronouncements about the nature of historical reality'.

Perhaps in the 1990s some may find it curiously archaic to highlight a moral imperative to explain why history matters. But to do so is by no means at odds with the 'new history' about which there has been so much debate, and indeed there are very strong reasons why it *should* be done.

Doing justice to the dead means getting the facts right. It can be a cue for the computers – they may be value free, their data is not: assize records of class-based justice in Georgian England or the manifests of Caribbean slave ships recording in dry prose fifty to sixty per cent mortality rates on hell-hole journeys from Africa. But whose facts – and whose dead? 'Some there be that have no memorial/who are perished as though they had never been' says the Book of Ecclesiasticus. Hannah Arendt tells us in her book on *Totalitarianism* that one of its worst curses was that it attempted not only to destroy people, but to obliterate their identity and memory.

The selection and presentation of history and its people is always, for good or ill, a political act. The past is enrolled either to justify or correct the present, and sometimes to promise an agenda for the future.

The dedication brought by Jewish scholars to the study of the

Holocaust – painstaking history in the most harrowing sense – is not only an act of pious remembrance for the dead but an affirmation for the living, of the determination of the Jewish people to survive, and, by extension and more controversially, of the State of Israel and its policies. The mammoth project now underway in the Soviet Union to track down the individual fates of millions who perished in Stalin's terror is driven by the same impulse and the increasing excavations of mass burial sites is its handmaid: archaeology as polemic. No symbolic act in the upheavals of Eastern Europe was more potent than the exhumation of Imre Nagy, the disgraced and executed Prime Minister of 1956 Hungary, and his triumphant hero's reburial in Budapest.

'Can these bones live?' asks the prophet Ezekiel in the Old Testament. The answer is yes – and in the 1990s they are being resurrected to confound the historical determinism of Big Brother. In ancient Egypt to deface the cartouches of the dead denied them their identity in a future life. But their historical imitators reckoned without the powers of memory, transmission and reconstruction with which history can tip the scales. Tradition, said Edmund Burke, was the democracy of the dead. 'Life's a bitch and then you die' is the more modern and nihilistic interpretation of the process. In a secularised culture that has dispensed with the last Judgement, history remains perhaps the most potent means we have for summoning up some sense of perspective on lives – individual or collective. If it takes us nearer Burke than 'life's a bitch', is it not something to be cherished?

But, it may be agreed, much of history does not occupy such an elevated plateau. Much of it in recent years has been history from below, of little people, not of Great Men (and the occasional Woman) or Great Crimes. The *Annales* school of French historians have enlisted climate, geography, flora and fauna as their walk-on characters in magisterial works such as Fernand Braudel's *Europe in the Age of Phillip II*. Such an approach is open to the objection that it is so all-embracing as to risk losing meaning or definition – history as *longue durée* may be uncharitably translated as a long hard slog.

But significantly the most successful communicator from the *Annales* group to a mass audience has been Emmanuel Le Roy Ladurie, whose book *Montaillou* has attained a cult status for medieval studies perhaps only rivalled in the fictional stakes by Umberto Eco's *Name of the Rose*. Why? Because for all the modernity of its methodology, *Montaillou*'s appeal remains that of story. It is a story perilously close to soap opera – an everyday tale of Cathar folk, albeit told in the course of an inquiry by the Inquisition. Like us, but not like us – but with at least some of the instincts that in other circumstances engross many in the neighbours of Ramsey Street or the regulars at *Coronation Street*'s Rovers Return (as indeed the Victorians lapped up the fraternity of Mr Pickwick and Dingley Dell). If such is the appeal, far from scoffing we should perhaps rejoice that history's appeal springs from the same roots of mass culture.

Is there more than a pleasure principle as a witness for the defence? It can persuasively be argued that the skills the study of history teaches – using evidence, assessing its importance and bias, constructing arguments and generalisations, picking out telling examples – contribute enormously to developing the informed, intelligent and model citizen. But intelligence is no guarantee of mortality. Of itself, all that would produce might be a group of clever devils – more adept at anti-social activities and at arguing their way out of trouble. A further step needs to be taken before those high claims can be made for history, and that takes us into the murky waters of empathy.

The buzz word of the last decade has been heritage. At its worst it means sanitised and cosy re-creations of the past in tourist settings – blood, sweat and tears missing (though sometimes authentic odours can be thoughtfully wafted in through an air-vent). Here looms a nightmare of twenty-first century Britain – clapped-out historical theme-park to the world. But at its best heritage means inheritance – that which lives in us and is passed on, in blood and bone, as real and relevant as DNA or chromosomes. We are born, grow, go to school. As we do so our awareness of inheritance – personal, family, local – fleshes out our historical senses. Looking at grandfather's historical novels, crawling over churchyard gravestones to find the earliest date were the first intimations of history for this six-year-old child growing up among the landscapes of Lowry.

At some point nation-state creeps in, which in this island brings both distinctiveness and danger. 'Men of England who *inherit*/rights that cost your sires their blood' but behind that crusty (and I suppose sexist) paean to Whig history imbued in school assembly and capable of any amount of satire à la Dennis Potter, lies a truth of continuity that can ennoble, so long as it is not idolised.

History's inheritances come in the plural – national, racial, social and sexual. That recognition can steer its students from tabloid to tolerance and the pluralism that is required to live in the post-cold war global village. Primary sources are what much of the new history has emphasised in the last thirty years – not just as the core of doctoral theses, but as material for pupils of twelve, thirteen and fourteen to grapple with. The tendency has been to think of computers and number-crunching the *Domesday Book* to report learnedly on land patterns after the conquest – *1066 and All That* on floppy disc. But many of the primary sources are letters, arguments, diaries – human beings putting up a front or letting down a guard – his-stories, less frequently hers but enough to recover the past from the received wisdoms of their establishments. I think, for instance, of Anne Lister – the high-spirited farmer's daughter in Regency Yorkshire – railing against her stereotypes and pouring out to her diary her passions for other women.

With such memoranda historians have reclaimed, almost without perhaps realising it, the concept of history as literature. At the other end of the scale, and much more self-consciously, they have been staking out literature as history – looking particularly in the golden age of sixteenth and seventeenth-century England, at the poets, playwrights and writers as points of entry to society's psychology via *King Lear, Richard II* or *Paradise Lost.*

Travel they say broadens the mind – there is a whole range of civic possibilities in historical 'travel' via the empathy that comes from familiarity with primary sources. They will never be achieved from the rote learning and parroting of dates, which *at best* could confirm us in a post-imperial smugness.

To understand all is *not* to forgive all. But without understanding how in the sixteenth century civilised and sophisticated men and women could condemn fellow beings to the flames for holding a different view of whether bread and wine literally became body and blood, our chances of spotting any contemporary sleep of reason and its ability to produce monsters will be impaired. I remember doing my own postgraduate research on popular religion at the time of the Reformation, trawling through first editions produced in the first half-century of printed books, looking at devotional images of the Virgin Mary and her crucified son, integrated with lyrics and texts of often considerable power and pathos.

How could this serene world of faith have crumbled? And then I came on one book with page after page of 'idolatrous' rubrics scored out by hand. A scribble in the margin by one of the pictures dripped savage sarcasm – 'ah – would there were many more of them – pretty, petty Gods'. To see the moment when Saul becomes Paul (or vice versa) and how, in the words of one historian, 'the image-makers became the image-breakers' sheds shafts of unsettling sunlight on today's orthodoxies and assumptions.

That medieval world which the Reformation destroyed was one of belief communicated by image. There is a curious sense, as we approach the second millennium, of the wheel come full circle. Perhaps logos and pictures are more easily accommodated than the printed word in the attention span of the three-minute culture. On the positive side not only has our sense of the image's importance at all levels in history grown apace – a process which *History Today* in a modest way has perhaps fostered in the past forty years – but the visual media now give a capacity to bring history alive for an audience many times that which would ever pick up a book by C.V. Wedgwood or Antonia Fraser. *Elizabeth R* and *The Six Wives of Henry VIII* brought on television a 'looking-glass' history – which is after all a form of 'empathy' – to millions who would have run a mile from it as a pedagogical concept. The same could be said of a Kenneth Clark or a Jacob Bronowski.

The power of such presentation has of course its dangers – particularly in history as drama – and not just to the subsequent careers of the actors involved. For many Glenda Jackson *is* Elizabeth I and Keith Michell, Henry VIII; they stamp their images on our mental currency more powerfully than a sheaf of monographs ever could. That is precisely why at the same time as making the bones live, historians must always be ready to deconstruct them and tell us – not least perhaps Government legislators too intent on meddling with minutiae – that there are no tablets from Sinai to produce an authorised version of history.

I have always found truth not just stranger but also more interesting than fiction, so it may not surprise that my final appeal to the court is for the liberating power history has on our imagination. The past *is* the bourn from which no traveller returns – even when we look at our own 'histories' from fifteen or twenty years ago it is at best a second cousin we see, sometimes a complete stranger. When history exercises its power over our imagination it is schizophrenic – we are there and not there, and our reaction to that failure is ambiguous. Perhaps that is why we are fascinated by the physical remains of other human beings from history. There is an atavistic thrill in peering at the body of Lindow Man, lifted from his Iron Age bog, the garotte still twisted round a leathery neck. There is pathos gazing at the features and the frayed cotton shirt of the young Victorian seaman, John Harrington, one of the first victims of Franklin's doomed 1847 expedition to find a North-West Passage, thawed out perfectly preserved from his icy grave in Arctic Canada just a couple of years ago.

These *memento mori* are the exceptions however. Imagination at its best in history will always outstrip even the worthiest attempt to recreate Viking Jorvik or a Victorian pit village. And in exercising that imagination history is capable of being the most democratic of disciplines. It is not just about glimpsing Henry VIII's armour or Good Queen Bess' four-poster and thinking romantically on the lives of the great and the good. It is about lying in your own bed at night in a 100-year-old house and wondering what the room looked like, who walked across it and what conversations floated up the stairs the first week of August – the last week of the old world – 1914. And wondering too if in a hundred years' time someone else will lie in the same room and try to conjure up *your* life.

CONTRIBUTORS

G.R. ELTON is the Regius Professor Emeritus of History in the University of Cambridge and author of many books, including *F.W. Maitland* (1985) and *The Parliament of England, 1559-81* (1986).

ROY PORTER is Senior Lecturer in the Social History of Medicine at the Wellcome Institute for the History of Medicine, London. He is the author of *English Society in the Eighteenth Century* (revised ed. 1990) and *The Democratizing of Desire: Creating the Consumer Society* (forthcoming).

KEITH ROBBINS is Professor of Modern History at the University of Glasgow and President of the Historical Association. He has been awarded a Winston Churchill Travelling Fellowship for 1990 to enable him to reflect on the teaching of British history in the context of current European developments.

WILLIAM LAMONT is Professor of History at the University of Sussex and author, with Christopher Hill and Barry Reay, of *The World of the Muggletonians* (1983).

J.C.D. CLARK is a Fellow of All Souls College, Oxford and the author of several books including *Revolution and Rebellion: State and Society in England in the Seventeenth and Eighteenth Centuries* (1986) and editor of *Ideas and Politics in Modern Britain* (1990).

CONRAD RUSSELL is Professor of British History at King's College, University of London and Ford Lecturer in English History at the University of Oxford, 1987-8.

JANET L. NELSON is a Reader in History at King's College, University of London, and author of *Politics and Ritual in Early Medieval Europe* (1986). She is also a convenor of the women's history seminar at the Institute of Historical Research.

ASA BRIGGS is Provost of Worcester College, Oxford and author of *Victorian People* (1954), *Victorian Cities* (1963), *Victorian Things* (1988), *The Social History of England* (1983) and four volumes of *The History*

NOV 1 3 1996

of Broadcasting in the United Kingdom (1961-1979 and forthcoming). He is a Fellow of the British Academy.

RAPHAEL SAMUEL is a tutor at Ruskin College, Oxford, a member of the editorial collective of *History Workshop Journal* and editor of *Patriotism: The Making and Unmaking of British National Identity* (1989).

F.M.L. THOMPSON retired as Director of the Institute of Historical Research, University of London in September 1990. He is President of the Royal Historical Society and editor of *The Cambridge Social History of Britain* (1990).

P.J. MARSHALL is Rhodes Professor of Imperial History at King's College, University of London and author of *The New Cambridge History of India Series II: 2 Bengal and the British Bridgehead* (1988). He was a member of the History Working Group on the National Curriculum.

JOHN MORRILL is Fellow and Senior Tutor at Selwyn College, Cambridge. His most recent book is *Oliver Cromwell and the English Revolution* (1990).

MICHAEL HUNTER is Reader in History at Birkbeck College, University of London and editor (with Robert Thorne) of *Change at King's Cross: from 1800 to the Present* (1990). He is co-author of *Avebury Reconsidered: From the 1660s to the 1990s* (forthcoming).

ALICE PROCHASKA is Secretary and Librarian at the Institute of Historical Research at the University of London. She was a member of the History Working Group on the National Curriculum.

ROBERT THORNE is an architectural and engineering historian who worked for the GLC Historic Buildings Division (later part of English Heritage) and now works for a firm of structural engineers. He is the editor (with Michael Hunter) of *Change at King's Cross: from 1800 to the Present* (1990).

GORDON MARSDEN is editor of *History Today* and a course tutor for the Open University. He is the editor of *Victorian Values: Personalities and Perspectives in Nineteenth-Century Society* (1990).